B2B MEANS
BACK TO BASICS

INTI
PUBLISHING

*Your Personal Growth
Is Our Personal Mission*

B2B Means Back to Basics

By Bill Quain, Ph.D.

Printed in the United States of America
First edition October, 2001

ISBN: 1-891279-08-4

Published by INTI Publishing, Inc.
Tampa, FL

Cover Design: Cherry Design
Layout: Parry Design Studio

intipublishing.com

The Internet Is Alive and Well!

When author and humorist Mark Twain discovered that a newspaper had mistakenly reported his death, Twain quipped, *"The rumors of my death have been greatly exaggerated!"*

We laugh at Twain's clever rejoinder, but exaggerations in the media are no laughing matter. Newspapers and TV newscasts are always looking for attention-grabbing headlines—even if they're not true. Bad news sells, so the media jump all over negative stories.

In the spring of 2000, the media struck gold—*the dot.com bubble burst!* Newspaper headlines blared the loss of billions in the stock market! Talking heads on the evening news crowed about the dot.com bomb.

If you listen to the media, the Internet is dead. Don't you believe it! To paraphrase Mark Twain, "The rumors of the Internet's death have been greatly exaggerated!"

No Big Surprise... Just Free Enterprise!

Sure, over the last few months, hundreds of Internet businesses have bit the dust. That's what happens in free enterprise. Ill-conceived and poorly managed companies lose money and eventually close up shop, whether they're located in a neighborhood strip mall... or on a worldwide virtual mall. There's just no remedy for bad business basics.

The fact that thousands of Internet businesses are going bust or are being gobbled up by the survivors is *no big surprise—it's just free enterprise.* You see, despite the negative news about the dot.com bomb, the Internet is alive and well and growing like gangbusters. *Forbes* magazine reports that estimated online sales in 2002 is $34 billion—equal to the entire U.S. retail market in 1940. Plus, e-commerce is growing at 35% a year, whereas traditional retail growth is about 4% to 5% per year. The Internet survivors are going great guns—because they're offering real products... earning real profits... and *practicing the real basics of business!*

What Are the Basics of Business?

What are the basics of business? As I see it, there are 10 basics of business that every successful enterprise must follow. These 10 basics of business apply to virtually any enterprise, but they're especially apropos to Internet-based businesses. That's why I named this book "B2B Means Back to Basics" (B2B is Internet shorthand for "business-to-business commerce").

You can't have a successful B2B... or B2C... or B2-anything else without following the basics of business. As an Independent Business Owner, there's no need for you to invent the basics. They've already been invented. Tested. And proved! That's the beauty of The Business— all you have to do is understand the basics... integrate those basics into your business plan... and then practice those basics over and over and over again.

Follow the basics and the money will follow—it doesn't get any more basic than that!

Dedication

To all the Independent Business Owners who understand that the road to success is always under construction.

Other Books by Dr. Bill Quain

- *Reclaiming the American Dream*

- *10 Rules to Break & 10 Rules to Make*

- *Pro-sumer Power!*

Contents

B2B Means "Back to Basics"

10 Basics of Business

Why I Wrote This Book

I wrote this book for all the Independent Business Owners (IBOs) using the Internet to build their businesses. My message is simple.

It's time for IBOs to get back on track! *It's time to get back to the basics!*

You see, somewhere along the way, some well-intentioned Business Builders took a detour. They got so excited about an amazing new tool called the Internet that they took their eye off the target. As a result, their businesses didn't grow as expected.

Hey, I can understand how that could happen. As a business owner myself, I know how easy it is to get off course. And as a college professor, consultant, and speaker for dozens of different businesses, I know how tempting it is to concentrate your energies so much on "selling the sizzle" that you neglect the steak. But in my 30-plus years as a business owner and marketing professor, I've come to realize that all successful businesses have one single thing in common:

Successful businesses are built on the basics. Everything else is just for show!

The Business is a Live Elephant, Not a Gray Wall!

"See the obvious," says management guru Peter Drucker. Problem is, sometimes we get so close to the obvious that it's not obvious anymore, and it begins to look like something entirely different!

If you stand too close to an elephant, for example, you could mistake one of its legs for a gray plaster wall. It's only by stepping back and changing your perspective that you can see the Big Picture.

Same goes for The Business. Some IBOs got so focused on "the big gray wall"—the computer with Internet access—that they took their eyes off the elephant—The Business! As a result, they mistook The Internet for The Business. Truth is, the Internet isn't The Business. The Internet is just one leg of The Business!

Once IBOs stand back from their computers and put things into perspective, they'll soon see that what they thought was a "wall" suddenly morphs into an elephant!

Time to Get Back to the Basics

Today, thanks to amazing technological breakthroughs, change is happening faster than ever. But no matter how much things change, the basics of business remain the same!

You see, there are certain proven principles that all business owners must practice in order for their businesses to grow, whether they're building their business in the Ice Age—or the Internet Age. The simple fact is, while business practices and tools change with the times, the proven principles of success are timeless.

As far as The Business is concerned, relationship-building is the most immutable, powerful principle of all. The first step in getting back to the basics is to understand that you're in the high-touch people business, not the hi-tech Internet business! If you don't touch people's hearts and souls, all the tech in the world won't do you any good.

The Big Picture Vs. the Nuts and Bolts

This book is designed to empower IBOs to re-energize their businesses by focusing their attention back on the tried-and-true basics of business.

A word of caution—this is NOT a how-to book. The best way to learn how to build the Business is to plug into and then follow the System put in place by your team leaders.

My purpose in writing this book is to paint the Big Picture in such a way that you have a better understanding of what needs to be done to achieve your Ultimate Goal— time and money freedom. When you get done with this book, you'll see The Business from a new perspective and in a new light. As a result, you'll have a better understanding of this "animal" called The Business—a renewed commitment to the opportunity—and a rekindled passion to the beauty of your dreams.

Remember—Big Dreams Are the Biggest Part of the Big Picture!

–Bill Quain, Ph.D.

10 Basics of Business

Introduction:

The Basics Are for Winners—Not Just Beginners!

When an archer misses the mark, he turns and looks for the fault within himself. Failure to hit the bulls-eye is never the fault of the target. To improve your aim—improve yourself!

—Gilbert Arland

Cradling a football in his arms as if it were a newborn baby, Vince Lombardi, the legendary coach of the Green Bay Packers football team, would officially open the first practice of each season with this proclamation:

"Gentlemen, this is a football!"

The players had heard Lombardi's opening line for years. Yet they would listen with rapt attention. Oh, sure, they all knew what a football was. These men had been playing football all their lives. But they understood that Lombardi's statement of the obvious was his way of reminding everyone of his number one principle for success:

1

Winning teams are built on the basics.

Lombardi harped on the basics more than anyone. His playbook was the simplest in the league. His game plans were the most predictable. On third down and short yardage, for example, every player on the opposing team knew that the Packers were going to run a sweep. Yet Paul Hornung or Jim Taylor would secure a first down anyway. Why? Because each offensive player would execute his basic assignment so well that the play would succeed. In fact, the basics succeeded so well that Green Bay dominated pro football for a decade, winning the first two Super Bowls ever played. Lombardi understood that the basics weren't just for beginners. *The basics were for winners!*

The Basics Put the FUN in "Fundamental"

Executing the basics may not look fancy. Or spectacular. But the basics enable you to get the results you want. And when it's all said and done, *results are the only thing that count!*

Lombardi's philosophy of coaching and his philosophy of life were one and the same: If you learn the basics and then execute those basics over and over and over, then nothing—and no one—can prevent you from achieving your goals in life.

Some people have the misconception that the basics are just for beginners. They think the basics are the first stage they have to go through before they can practice the really fancy moves. Nothing could be further from the truth! The reason successful people reach the very top of their professions is that they practice the basics over and over.

Tiger Woods, the great young golfer, is a perfect example. At age 21, Woods won the most prestigious golf tournament in the world, the Masters, by a record 18 strokes under par. His mastery of one of golf's most difficult courses was so convincing that the tournament took the unprecedented measure of re-designing Augusta National, the site of the Masters Tournament, to make it more difficult. The re-design effort became known as "Tiger-proofing" the course.

So what did Woods do to celebrate his win? He scheduled months of work with a golf coach to rebuild his swing. Why? Because he felt his swing was getting sloppy and he wanted to "return to the basics."

Think about it—here's a guy who just dominated a field of the world's greatest golfers, and he dedicated the next six months of his life to getting back to the basics. What does that tell you about the importance of learning and practicing the basics? It tells me what I told you in my opening remarks: *Successful businesses [and athletic careers] are built on the basics. Everything else is just for show!*

First the Razzle-Dazzle... Then the Fizzle

Vince Lombardi and Tiger Woods reached the top of their professions by concentrating on the "boring old basics," as opposed to crowd-pleasing "razzle-dazzle" antics. Why? Because as true professionals, they were focused on accomplishing their goal of winning, as opposed to looking good in front of the cameras. And winning requires mastering the basics and repeating them over and over again.

Oh, sure, razzle-dazzle looks great on ESPN's 30-second highlights. But all too often razzle-dazzle ends up with a fizzle: The 360-degree slam dunk caroms off the rim... the between-the-legs tennis shot sails out of bounds... and dozens of poorly managed dot.com start-ups flare out like cheap bottle rockets on the Fourth of July!

Look, it's human nature to be attracted to new and exciting things. Everybody loves the pre-game fireworks. Everybody loves the behind-the-back pass (even when a simple bounce pass would get the job done with a lot less risk of failure). But when all is said and done, razzle-dazzle doesn't win games. It's the basics that win games. And it's the basics that grow businesses.

Why the Basics Are Essential to THE BUSINESS

The basics are important to every human endeavor. Think of the basics as the foundation of a structure. In order for the structure to endure, it must be built on a solid foundation. Whether you're trying to win consistently at a sport... raise happy, well-adjusted children... master a musical instrument... or grow a successful business—you have to build your enterprise on a solid foundation of basics. If you neglect the basics, your building begins to crack and sag, and unless you shore up the foundation, it's only a matter of time before the building falls down around you!

Now, the basics are important in any business. But in **THE BUSINESS, the basics are everything!** You see, the key to success in The Business is to keep things simple. Keep things duplicatable. See the people. Show the plan. Teach others to do the same. Doesn't get anymore basic than that, does it?

Razzle-dazzle doesn't work in The Business. Never has, never will. In The Business, the basics and The Business are one and the same. Doing the basics is to The Business what breathing is to humans. Stop breathing and you stop living. Stop doing the basics, and you stop doing The Business.

Oh, sure, the longer people work The Business, the more they learn the "tricks of the trade" that help them grow their organizations. But when IBOs start putting more emphasis on the "tricks" than the "basics," well, that's when the foundation starts to weaken and the cracks and sags start to appear. As H. Jackson Brown observed in *Life's Little Instruction Book,* "Don't learn the tricks of the trade. Learn the trade."

Unfortunately, some IBOs failed to heed Brown's advice—they started focusing on the "trick" of hi-tech Internet and started ignoring the basics of their hi-touch business. It wasn't long before the cracks started to appear and IBOs businesses began to sag.

The Internet: The Ultimate Razzle-Dazzle

The biggest problem with the basics is that, well, *they're so basic!* The basics aren't glamorous. The basics aren't new and exciting. The basics are dependable, routine and predictable, sort of like parents. (And as our children frequently remind us, *"Parents are, like, s-o-o-o-o boring!"*)

When The Business transitioned to the Internet, some IBOs took their eyes off the "Boring Old Basics" to stare at the glamorous new World Wide Web. They became hypnotized! Jaws dropped and sparks began to fly! It was like a movie star visiting your small town and asking YOU out on a date! Compared to the movie star called the Internet, the basics seemed more old-fashioned and boring than ever before! As a result, some IBOs got swept up in the razzle-dazzle of the Internet and temporarily turned their backs on the basics. They mistook the sizzle of the Internet for the steak of The Business. As a result, hi-touch relationships took a back seat to hi-tech hysteria.

It didn't take long before the razzle-dazzle of the Internet started to fizzle. The more the basics were relegated to the back seat, the more some businesses suffered. The good news is that all is not lost. Like the parable of the Prodigal Son, you can come home to your always-dependable parents, the basics.

Look, if you were one of the people who was dazzled by the pyrotechnics of the Internet, don't feel like the Lone Ranger. I tried to float on the dot.com bubble, too. Invested some of my hard-earned money in Internet high-flyers with no earnings run by 20-year-old college dropouts. It was hard NOT to get carried away by the Internet hysteria. But it was only a matter of time before the dot.com bubble was burst by the basics of business. Like a lot of investors, I got burned when the dot.bomb exploded.

The Internet Is a Tool, Not a Business

Now, please don't misunderstand—I'm not down on the Internet. If anything, I'm a bigger fan of the Internet than ever before. I've always said that the Internet is a great tool—maybe the greatest tool ever invented. But there's a difference between using the Internet as a tool and using the Internet as a business model. A BIG DIFFERENCE! Let me explain:

Right now the Internet is in the midst of the biggest shakeout in the history of free enterprise. Almost every pure-play Internet start-up is struggling to stay alive. As I write this, almost 600 Internet businesses have closed their doors in the past 12 months—and more are sure to follow. As a result of the shakeout, investors have lost trillions of dollars (and counting) as the hot air continues to leak out of the over-inflated Internet balloon.

Now, compare the "tech wreck" of the Internet start-ups to traditional companies that are using the Internet as a tool. That's a whole different story! *Companies that effectively use the Internet as a tool are still growing like gangbusters!* Walmart.com and Target.com are going great guns. Southwest Airlines is on track to sell $1 billion worth of tickets on their website in 2001.

Why are some bricks-and-mortar companies flourishing on the Internet while the dot.com start-ups are dropping like flies? Because instead of trying to become an Internet business, savvy traditional companies are sticking to their core businesses while using the reach, speed, and connectivity of the Internet to increase productivity. Consider what using the Internet as a tool can do for companies: The Net can save valuable time and money. Expand the customer base. Eliminate fees to middlemen. Offer shopping convenience. Enhance interactive communication. Provide information and training. The list goes on and on.

Unfortunately, some IBOs became so enamored with the Internet that they made the mistake of acting like they were a start-up Internet company instead of a savvy bricks-and-mortar company using the Internet as a tool. The more the IBOs got wrapped up in the Internet part of the business, the farther away they got from the basics.

Better Tools Make a Better Carpenter

Here's an analogy that will illustrate what I mean when I say it's crucial to treat the Internet as a tool instead of a business model.

Let's say you were a carpenter in the 1950s. You're a hard worker. You have a great reputation. Got lots of clients. A handsaw is one of your major tools. You can cut a 2x4 quicker than anyone with your handsaw. Along comes a great new invention, the table saw. It doesn't take you long to realize that a table saw will make you much more productive. So you take the plunge and invest in a table saw.

So, let me ask you a question. Now that you've made the decision to switch from a handsaw to a table saw, do you start acting like you're in the table saw business? *Of course not!* That would be absurd! You'd still be a carpenter, whether you're using a handsaw or a table saw.

The basics of your carpentry business haven't changed, have they? You'd still be building houses. That's what carpenters do. But with a table saw, you'd be a much more productive builder.

Parallel the carpenter analogy to The Business. Instead of building houses, you're building a network of IBOs. You've made the switch from the old "handsaw" way of doing business to the ultimate "table saw"—The Internet. Just because you've switched tools doesn't mean you've switched businesses, wouldn't you agree? Like the carpenter, you're still a builder. The Internet is a tool to help you become a more productive builder of networks. The Net is a *means to an end,* not an end in itself!

Give Credit to the Leadership

Look, the leadership did the right thing when they transitioned The Business to the Internet. They had the vision to see that the Internet could be a great Business-building tool. It was a brilliant move. A necessary move. And a timely move. As with any quantum leap, there were some growing pains. That's to be expected. But in the long run, The Business—and you—will be better off for adding the Internet to your tool belt.

As the smoke from the dot.bomb explosion clears, you'll see that the leadership has successfully created a business model that is lasting... durable... and flexible. Only the best of the best will survive the shakeout on the Internet, and The Business has not only survived—it has thrived! *The future is so bright you need sunglasses!*

Final Comment

As I said earlier, this book is *not* a step-by-step, how-to-build-your-business training manual. I'm not in a position to do that. My role as an outside consultant to businesses is to identify problems and offer solutions, not to tell companies how to perform their daily operations. I leave that up to the leaders. Your leaders will work with you on the daily actions necessary for success.

Think of The System as the road map to follow on your journey to success. Now think of this book as your eyeglasses, helping to bring the Big Picture into focus. Once you focus on the 10 basics of business, you'll have a much clearer picture of what roads to follow to get you to your ultimate destination—a small, exclusive community known as Time and Money Freedom!

Some IBOs without eyeglasses took a wrong turn on the road to success. They thought they were taking the shortest route to Time and Money Freedom. But because their vision was blurry, they inadvertently took a detour instead. Maybe you were one of those who took a detour. This book will bring your road map into sharp focus! Once that happens, you'll be able to see clearly where you are and how best to get to your destination.

When all is said and done, there's no substitute for practicing the basics of business. That's where your focus should be. If you accidentally took a wrong turn in The Business, that's okay. It's not too late to make a U-turn and get back on the road to riches again.

Here's a little poem I made up for you to recite to yourself during your journey. It'll remind you to stay focused, keep your eyes on the road, and to never lose sight of the basics.

Whether it's the "Net"... or whether it's not... Business is business (in case you forgot)!

Understand What Business You're <u>Really</u> In!

I think a lot of people initially thought that the "e" in e-business was more important than the business part. Business fundamentals haven't changed, and a lot of investors lost sight of that—and are paying for it.

—Michael Dell
Founder, Chairman, and CEO of Dell Computer

"What business are you in?"

You may be thinking, "That's a silly question if I ever heard one!"

Actually, "What business are you in?" is a profound question. In fact, **understanding what business you're really in is the single most important basic in all of business!**

The best way to explain the importance of knowing what business you're *really* in is to tell you about an incident that happened to Mark McCormack, founder and CEO of IMG, the largest sports agency in the world.

McCormack was returning from Europe on the Concorde when he spotted Andre Heiniger, president of Rolex. McCormack walked up the aisle to Heiniger's seat, extended his hand, introduced himself, and asked innocently, "How's the watch business?"

Heiniger stared icily at McCormack before replying coldly, "I wouldn't know how the watch business is doing. I'm not in the watch business. *I'm in the luxury business.*"

Now, think about Heiniger's response for a second. If someone had asked me what business Rolex was in, I'd have said the watch business without hesitation. After all, Rolex makes wristwatches. But so does Timex. And Seiko. Is Rolex in competition with those two watchmakers? Not by a long shot!

You see, Timex and Seiko are in the watch business. They sell wristwatches in discount stores for as little as $20. Most Rolex watches, on the other hand, cost thousands of dollars each—and some custom-made models cost hundreds of thousands! Rolex watches are sold in jewelry stores or by private dealers. If you want a watch, buy a Timex. *But if you want to make a statement about status, power, or wealth, then Rolex is the watch for you!*

The Power of Knowing What Business You're In

Heiniger is a perfect example of a man who knows exactly what business he's in. If Heiniger had decided that

Rolex were in the watch business, he would lower his prices to compete against Timex and Seiko and dozens of other watchmakers. Rolex could easily introduce an affordable wristwatch to sell to the mass market. But that would tarnish Rolex's image as a luxury item that only the rich and beautiful can afford. By remaining in the luxury business, Rolex has a great marketing position—they can sell one watch for $10,000, whereas Timex has to sell 500 watches at $20 apiece to bring in the same revenue.

Let me ask you, if you could be the CEO of a watch company, which one would you rather head up? Mass-market Timex? Or luxury-market Rolex? I'd choose Rolex in the blink of an eye because they virtually own the luxury market, whereas competitors are breathing down Timex's neck!

When you think about it, how you answer the question, *"What business are you really in?"* will impact all of your business decisions because it defines the parameters of your business. It sets your agenda. Establishes your goals. Guides your daily thoughts and actions. And determines where you spend your time and money. Understanding what business you're *really* in establishes the paradigm for everything you do. It's the vision... the road map... and the mission statement—all rolled into one!

How Two Big Thinkers Changed the World

To fully comprehend the power of knowing what business you're in, let me tell you how two legendary businessmen, Ray Kroc and Henry Ford, transformed two major industries by understanding better than their contemporaries what business they were *really* in.

Before the McDonald brothers met Ray Kroc, they owned and operated three very successful fast-food restaurants in California. The brothers thought of themselves as being in the restaurant business. Kroc expanded McDonald's from a local restaurant business to an international empire by answering the question "What business are you *really* in?" very differently from the brothers. Kroc's answer was "McDonald's is in the franchising business." By expanding the parameters of the business, he grew McDonald's from three local stores to the biggest fast-food chain in the world.

Henry Ford did likewise. When cars were first introduced, they were hand built and very expensive. Only rich people could afford them. But Henry Ford didn't want to cater just to the rich. He envisioned manufacturing a car for the masses. So when Ford asked himself the question "What business are you *really* in?" his answer was "Ford Motor Company is in the mass-production business." As a result of his expanded vision, Ford invented the moving assembly line that reduced a car's assembly time from 12 hours to 93 minutes, and, in the process, reduced the price of a car so that even a working-class family could afford a brand-new Model T Ford.

What Business Are You In?

Now it's your turn to answer the question, "What business are you in?"

Many IBOs would answer, "The distribution business"... or "The e-commerce business." Both of these answers are correct to a degree, but they don't capture the essence of The Business. They don't describe what business you're *really* in.

Here's my answer to the question "What business are you *really* in?"

You're in the business of building business builders.

Think about it—the most successful people in The Business—the Diamonds—are the best business builders, wouldn't you agree? That's because they understand that the biggest profits in The Business come from a whole bunch of people, each consuming a little bit of product every single month. The Diamonds understand that the only way to build huge organizations is through duplication—building The Business by teaching others how to become business builders. That's the way solid, profitable organizations grow—Diamonds building Diamonds building Diamonds.

Now, compare Diamonds who're in the business of building business builders to IBOs who think they're in the retailing business. IBOs who think they're in the retailing business will focus most of their efforts on personally selling products and services. Now, let me say that retailing is a good thing. Retailing is necessary. Retailing is profitable.

But if you're in the business of building business builders, retailing is a just a natural by-product of working The Business, just as selling hamburgers is a natural by-product of McDonald's franchising. Ray Kroc *maximized* his opportunity by expanding McDonald's through franchising. Henry Ford maximized his opportunity through mass production. Likewise, Diamonds are maximizing their opportunity by building business builders.

17

The Problem with Thinking You're in the e-Commerce Business

Unfortunately, when The Business transitioned to the Internet, some IBOs naturally assumed they were now in the e-commerce or B2C business.

Bad assumption! Here's why:

If you're in the business of building business builders, the Internet is a *means to an end*—not an end in itself. Unfortunately, some IBOs lost sight of that. They got so caught up in the hype of this awesome new technology that they mistook the Internet for The Business. As a result, they stopped doing the time-tested basics of business and started trying to reinvent the wheel.

I can see why IBOs got off message and strayed off course. The Internet is a dazzling tool. Perhaps the most powerful tool ever invented. But the Internet is still a tool, plain and simple.

Ironically, the Internet isn't the first technology to dramatically impact The Business. IBOs took to fax machines, cell phones, and voice mail like a duck to water, and The Business exploded along with these technological breakthroughs. But when IBOs started using fax machines, they didn't suddenly start thinking they were in the fax machine business, did they? No—they immediately recognized fax machines for what they were—a tool to help them build their business more efficiently.

Not so with the Internet. The Internet was such a disruptive technology that it disrupted the proven way of building The Business – that is, people talking to people, building The Business one relationship at a time.

Remember—the answer to "What business are you *really* in?" sets the parameters for all your thoughts and actions. Because some IBOs started thinking and acting like they were in the e-commerce business, they started *concentrating on the hi-tech Internet part of the business while neglecting the hi-touch people part of the business.* As a result, computers and software and websites took precedence over people and relationships and personal growth. *Big mistake!*

Time to "Dance with the One Who Brung You"

When all is said and done, The Business is a people business. Without people, The Business doesn't even exist. People are the lifeblood of The Business. Not computers. People. As my uncle used to say, "It's time to dance with the one who brung you." People are the ones who "brung you to the dance," and they'll be the ones who help you reach your Ultimate Goal of time and money freedom.

Well, it's time to dance with your date before it's too late! It's time to begin at the beginning... to get back to basics... and to understand that the business you're really in is the business of building business builders.

As you will learn in the coming chapters, that means knowing your competition. Filling in the gaps. Finding out what your partners want. Looking for big problems! Planning your work. Working your plan. And adding value to everything you do!

As long as you're in the business of building business builders, you'll understand that caring and sharing are the backbone of The Business. Always have been. Always will be. Never lose sight of that and you'll be in The Business for as long as there is a Business!

Know Your Competition

In business, the competition will nip at your heels if you keep running. But if you stand still, they'll swallow you.

–William Knudsen, Jr.
Chairman, Ford Motor Company

T here's an old saying here in the States: *"Tell me who you hang out with and I'll tell you who you are."* In other words, if someone knows your friends, they also know you because friends share the same basic values.

Business is just the opposite. In business, you're not known by your friends—you're known by your competition. Coke vs. Pepsi. Ford vs. Chevy. The Home Depot vs. Lowe's. NBC vs. ABC. McDonald's vs. Burger King.

Many businesses have failed because they didn't understand who their competition was. Conversely, some products have THRIVED because the manufacturer or promoter suddenly realized who the competition *really* was.

Perrier Explodes by Rethinking the Competition

Perrier water is a perfect example of a company that succeeded by redefining their competition. Twenty years ago, Perrier marketed itself as an alternative to alcoholic beverages. At the time, Perrier was sold mostly in liquor stores. They defined their competition as all alcoholic beverages.

One day the executives at Perrier decided to EXPAND THEIR MARKET. They decided to market Perrier as an alternative to soft drinks, instead of an alternative to alcohol. Getting back to this simple basic—know your competition—turned Perrier into an "overnight" success.

Within months of repositioning their product, Perrier's bottled water business exploded! Soon, Perrier was available in every supermarket and convenience store in the world. The price was reduced to compete with soda. Today, the market for bottled water is the fastest growing segment of the beverage industry and second in sales only to soft drinks. And Perrier is the biggest player.

Higher Convenience Means Higher Prices

Who do you consider your competition in The Business? If your answer is Wal-Mart or Target or the supermarkets, you're in for trouble! Why? Because the "big box" deep-discount stores compete on price. Their goal is to sell LOTS of stuff at very small profit margins. Big grocery store chains, for example, plan on earning TWO PERCENT on every item they sell. That means that for every dollar they spend on products to stock the shelves, they net two pennies. TWO PENNIES!

How do grocery stores stay in business with such skinny profit margins? By selling BILLIONS of products in thousands of stores all over the world, that's how. Their strategy is to make their money on volume sales. Their competition is doing the same thing. It's a cutthroat business, that's for sure.

Now, it's crucial to understand that not every business competes on low prices. In fact, some businesses are able to charge ABOVE RETAIL PRICES and still do TONS of business! Convenience stores are a perfect example. Let's say the price for a quart of Borden's milk at the local Pak 'N Save superstore is $1. But you're in a hurry. So you pull into the local 7-11 convenience store and grab some milk while you're gassing up. How much is that same quart of Borden's? At least $2, maybe more.

How do convenience stores get away with charging customers double or triple the price they'd pay at the local supermarket? Simple. Customers shop at convenience stores to save time, not money. As a result, the time customers save is priced into each product.

You see, convenience stores charge sky-high prices and still do LOTS of business because they practice Business Basics #2: *They know their competition!* Convenience stores understand that they're NOT competing with the superstores on price. Convenience stores compete with other convenience stores (that's why you see a convenience store on every other corner), not with supermarkets. Convenience stores want to make it EASY for you to buy. Easy... but definitely NOT cheap!

If consumers allow convenience stores to charge 100% to 200% more than grocery stores, then it stands to reason that the lowest price is not the only thing that motivates shoppers, isn't that true? People are also motivated to save time and effort and to reduce stress. And they'll pay a rich premium for those privileges.

What Price, Opportunity?

So, let's get back to the original question. In The Business, who is *your* competition? It's not Wal-Mart or Kmart, that's for sure. If you try competing with those guys on price, you'll lose every time. Is it the convenience stores? No, although you're getting closer, because it's a lot more convenient to order a product online and have it shipped to your door than it is to shop at Circle K or 7-11.

But if you're in the business of building business builders, you're not really in competition with any retail stores. You're not even in competition with any e-commerce websites. Why? Because they can't offer shoppers what you have to offer. You see, there's something priced into the cost of your products that no one else has.

What you have priced into your products is opportunity!

Think about what I just said—opportunity is priced into your products. Wow! That's a powerful statement. Does Piggly Wiggly offer opportunity in the cleaning products aisle? NO! Does The Gap offer opportunity in their "Summer Clearance" section? NO! Does Circuit City offer opportunity in their personal computer department? NO!

How about Sears? Tire Kingdom? Sam's Club? NO! NO! NO!

But you can offer opportunity along with your products and services, can't you? You can offer the opportunity to earn anywhere from a couple hundred extra bucks a month working part-time... to creating total time and money freedom working full-time.

Does any other retailer or wholesaler you know offer the same kind of thing at ANY PRICE? Not on your life.

The Business Is a Very Different Animal with Very Different Competition

OK, we've established that your competition isn't the stores. Wise decision, because Wal-Mart and Kmart are *very good* at what they do. And what they do is create huge warehouse-like stores and lure people in with low prices. You don't have a chance in that environment. But because The Business offers opportunity, it's a very different animal from retailing. VERY DIFFERENT. As a result, you have very different competition than retail stores have. VERY DIFFERENT! Let me explain what I mean by asking a few simple questions.

Why do people go to work each day? To get money so that they can buy the things that make them happy, correct?

Do you think most people enjoy their jobs? No.

Would most people jump at the opportunity to earn more money? Yes.

Would most people jump at the opportunity to own their own business, set their own hours, and work from home? Yes.

Would most people prefer to create ongoing residual income instead of trading their time for money? Yes.

So, considering that you're offering people the opportunity to earn money in their own business, who's your competition? Your competition—is low-paying jobs. Your competition is dead-end careers. Your competition is high-stress professions. Your competition is time clocks. Your competition is demanding bosses. Your competition is no recognition. Your competition is work cubicles. Your competition is increasing workloads (with no increase in pay). Your competition is cutthroat corporate politics. Your competition is no time for the family. *That's who your competition is—all of the above, AND MORE!*

Competing Against Low Expectations

Here's the bottom line. Because opportunity is priced into your products, you're not competing against a store's low prices. You're competing against *people's low expectations!*

Think about it. Everybody wants more money and more time to enjoy the things that money can buy, isn't that true? But instead of increasing their income to accommodate the size of their dreams, most people deflate their dreams to accommodate the size of their income. In a word, most people settle for less instead of reaching for more. They whittle down their expectations so that they won't be disappointed with what they have.

That's why I say that what you're ultimately competing against are people's low expectations! It's true! It can be tough to convince someone who has always worked for a salary that they can earn residual income. It can be tough to convince someone who has always been *dependent* on an employer for a paycheck that they can become an *Independent Business Owner!* Fact is, the hardest part isn't convincing someone that there's a better way to create wealth—the hardest part is getting people to *convince themselves* that they can make it happen!

The Business of Building Business Builders

Now are you beginning to see why I chose to list "You're in the Business of Building Business Builders" as Business Basic #1? If your competition isn't low prices but low expectations, then you need to learn how to build people up so that they can build up their businesses, wouldn't you agree?

Business Basic #1 and #2 go hand in hand—your job is to build people up so that you can build the business together! In The Business, you develop PEOPLE, not products. Yes, you're still moving products. That's where the money comes from. But while you're helping your new people *move products,* you're also helping them *remove their self-imposed limitations!*

You see, you're adding a different kind of value than convenience stores (who add time to people's lives) or Rolex watches (who add status to people's lives). *You're adding opportunity to people's lives!* You're adding time and money freedom. You're adding personal growth. You're adding friendship. You're adding a positive attitude. You're adding hope. You're adding leadership. You're

27

adding a values-based community of BELIEVERS AND ACHIEVERS!

You're building business builders. You're developing long-term relationships with people. That's a vastly different business from retail stores or e-commerce sites!

Stores are only interested in *taking* people's money.

But you're interested in *giving* people confidence... skills... direction... and support. But most of all, you're giving people an opportunity to own their own lives by owning their own businesses. You can't put a price on that!

Do Whatever It Takes to Realize Your Dream!

The person with big dreams is more powerful than one with all the facts.

–from *Life's Little Instruction Book*

Have you ever had a conversation with someone who asks you, "What do you do?" Usually, they mean, "What job do you have?"

I was recently asked the "What do you do?" question by a man I met in an airport while waiting on a delayed flight. He told me he worked as a technician for a big company. He was just returning from a special job that paid him lots of overtime. The man was very excited about the extra money he'd made and made it a point to tell me about all the ways he intended to spend his windfall. Then, when the conversation hit a lull, he asked me THE QUESTION.

"What do you do?" he asked perfunctorily.

"I do whatever it takes," I replied. "In fact, that's my company motto."

"You do whatever it takes to do WHAT?" he asked.

"I do whatever it takes to realize my dreams," I said.

The man looked at me like I was a little crazy. Then he backed up a step and made some lame excuse about why he had to go. I watched as he sidled up to another unsuspecting passenger. I checked my watch. Sure enough, within five minutes I heard him pop THE QUESTION:

"What do you do?"

Tell Me What You Do, and I'll Tell You What You're Worth

The What-do-you-do? man wasn't used to the answer I gave him. It was unsettling to him. Confusing. He wanted me to tell him what I did so that he could get a good "read" on me. The answer he was looking for was a job description, as in, "I'm a doctor"... or "I'm a banker"... or "I'm a car mechanic."

If I told him my job, he'd start making assumptions about my lifestyle. That's just the way people are. You can almost see their mental wheels turning. Goes something like this:

"Okay, this guy I just met tells me he's a barber. Means he makes about $30,000 a year, if he's lucky. Probably drives a used Toyota with a dented front fender. Wife works to help pay the bills. Kids go to public school. Hates what he does but can't afford to retire."

You know, it's not fair that people make huge, sweeping generalizations about others based on their jobs.

30

It's just not fair. But that's not the worst part. *The worst part is that all too often, the generalizations are right!*

Wrongful Death Settlements

Actually, making big generalizations about people based on a little information isn't necessarily a bad thing. In fact, the entire insurance industry is built on sweeping generalizations—and insurance is one of the biggest, most profitable industries in the world.

Over the years, insurance companies have compiled huge data bases called "actuary tables" that enable the insurers to accurately predict people's futures based on a small amount of information. For example, all you have to tell a life insurance company is your age, sex, and occupation, and they'll be able to predict with 90% accuracy how much longer you'll live. Amazing, isn't it? That's how life insurance companies make their money— they're betting that you'll live long enough to pay them more in premiums than they'll have to pay out in death benefits after you die.

Lawyers also rely heavily on actuary tables to help them calculate "wrongful death settlements." For example, let's say a 25-year-old forklift operator earning $25,000 a year gets in an accident at work and dies. His family hires an attorney, who files a wrongful death suit against the employer. The attorney consults the actuary tables and determines that if the man had lived, he would have earned $25,000 a year plus benefits for 40 years, which, adjusted for inflation, comes to well over a million dollars. The lawyer sues the employer for $1.2 million, the total lifetime WORTH of the forklift driver.

No Place for Dreams on Actuary Charts

The reason I'm telling you about actuary tables is to reinforce the point of the opening story about the man who asked, "What do you do?" The point is that what we DO equals what we're WORTH, whether we like it or not! That's why I told the man, *"I do whatever it takes to realize my dreams."*

You see, I know that dreams can't be entered into an actuary table! It would mess everything up! Can you see an actuary trying to predict Bill Gates' or Michael Dell's total WORTH based on an actuary table?

"Let's see," says the actuary as he fondles his calculator. "Mr. Gates and Mr. Dell are college dropouts who started their own businesses before they were 20 years old. According to the actuary tables, they have a 1% chance of founding profitable companies. Which means they'll likely be working for someone else within two years. Therefore, I anticipate they'll earn an average of $35,000 a year, which is the annual salary for a high school graduate with two years of college, for the next 45 years, putting their total lifetime worth at $2 million, maximum." *OOOPS! The actuary's calculation was only off by $99.8 BILLION!*

Actuaries HATE guys like Gates and Dell. Hate 'em! Why? Because guys like Gates and Dell have dreams so big that they won't fit in the actuary table's narrow columns, that's why!

Truth is, the total WORTH of a car mechanic or a pediatrician who REMAINS in their chosen occupation until they retire can be calculated within a few thousand dollars. That's just a fact. Actuaries know that the best predictor of a person's future is their past. As my friend Burke Hedges always says, "Keep doing what you've always done, and you'll keep getting what you've always gotten."

I call this kind of behavior *"a wrongful life settlement."* When someone settles for the "security" of working for someone else for the rest of their lives, that's a wrongful life settlement. The only way to turn a wrongful life settlement into a rightful reward is to have a big dream and then do whatever it takes to accomplish it. "Do whatever it takes to realize your dream"—that's not just a business basic. That's a LIFE BASIC!

It's the Small Things That Kill You

I once heard a speaker who opened his talk by asking the question, "How many people here have ever been bitten by an elephant?"

No one raised their hand. Then he asked, "How many people here have ever been bitten by a mosquito?" Everybody raised their hands.

"You see," said the speaker, "over the years, millions of people have died from diseases transmitted by mosquito bites, while no one has ever died from an elephant bite. *Just proves that it's the little things that kill you!"*

It's the same way in business. Very few businesses are killed by the big things. It's the little things that really kill you. You know, the little distractions, such as the negative thoughts... daily procrastinations... annoying details... sick kids... car won't start... computer crashes. These daily distractions are the little things that add up to THE BIG THING that eventually drags you down!

That's why it's so important to have a big dream. It protects you from the little distractions that nip at you all day long. Think of your dream as mosquito repellent! You slather yourself all over with your dream, and those annoying little mosquitoes just refuse to land on you. They just buzz you and then fly off to feast on someone who forgot to lather up with his dream that morning! You see, a dream gives you focus. A dream reminds you to ignore the little things. If you're focused on a dream—the goal—then all those annoyances will simply buzz off.

Focus on the Finish Line, Not the Hurdle

Try this experiment. Look up from your book right now and focus on something on the wall. Stare at it. Look at every detail of that thing. Soon, you will only see that ONE thing. Everything else in the room will fade away. (Try it!—it really works!)

Dreams are the same way. If you concentrate on them, the other stuff happening around you just doesn't come into the picture! The distractions don't go away. They just fade out of sight. This is an important point to remember. People will say, "Well, I focused on my dream, but those other things were still there."

Of course they were still there! Just because you have a dream doesn't mean that the rest of the world is going to leave you alone. In fact, your friends and family may even get MORE intense in their efforts to distract you from your dream. But, if you focus on your dream, those little

34

annoyances will have less EFFECT on you. Before long, the distractions seem invisible.

Hurdles Are Designed for Jumping

In my speeches and consulting to companies, I tell my audience to think of themselves as Olympic hurdlers. That means your focus should be on the finish line, not the first hurdle. If all of your attention is on the hurdle, then it gets even taller. And wider. You look down the track and the hurdles seem to have multiplied from a few... to hundreds!

But if you stay focused on the finish line, then you understand that the hurdles are just something you and everyone else in the race has to jump over on the way to realizing the dream of winning the gold medal!

Success isn't an absence of hurdles—success depends on how smoothly you negotiate over the hurdles. In business and in life, the hurdles are a given. They're gonna be there, you can count on it! If you plan on quitting the race every time you come to a hurdle, then you're in for some major disappointments in your life. MAJOR DISAPPOINTMENTS—because you're never going to accomplish ANYTHING! The most successful people aren't the best hurdle removers. The most successful people are the best hurdle jumpers! Never forget that.

Dream Building — A Team Sport

I'm a big believer in setting yourself up for success. The best way to set yourself up to realize your dream is to share it with others. If you keep your dreams to yourself, it's too easy to make excuses. Bring other people into your dream circle. Share with each other. Know why you're in The Business, and, just as importantly, know why your TEAM MEMBERS are in The Business.

Like charity, dream building begins at home. Share your dreams with your spouse and children. If they don't respond to your dreams, ask them what THEIR dreams are. If you have a problem getting support from a spouse, try to get them dreaming as well. As I said, pursuing your dream is like running a hurdle race. But if only one spouse has a dream, the race is even tougher! It's like running a hurdle race UPHILL!

If you have a dream but your spouse doesn't, don't throw in the towel! It may simply be a case of two individuals being in different dream stages. My wife, Jeanne, and I have found ourselves in different dream stages during our 17 years of marriage.

For example, in the summer of 2000, my then six-year-old daughter, Kathleen, was diagnosed with Type 1 diabetes. The family was traveling on vacation at the time, so we definitely had some tall "hurdles" to jump. Jeanne and I sent our other daughter, Amanda, to stay with her grandparents and then spent the rest of our vacation at the Children's Hospital of Philadelphia learning to deal with this new situation.

It was time to re-evaluate our game plan for realizing our dreams. Because Jeanne was the at-home parent, she would be taking primary responsibility for Kathleen's daily regimen of insulin shots and blood tests. Fortunately, years ago we'd made the decision for Jeanne to stay at home while the kids were in school, so Jeanne was able to care for Kathleen full time and to teach others (like the school nurse and Kathleen's teachers) how to care for her, as well.

This new routine would dictate a major change in our lifestyle, but we were certainly willing to make the changes. It also meant a change in our dream process. Jeanne and I had always been dream partners. We both liked setting big, specific goals. One night, we talked about our new situation. We recognized that Jeanne would have to be in the Survival Mode for a while so she could concentrate on Kathleen's immediate medical needs.

But, we didn't want to lose sight of our long-term dreams. We agreed that I would concentrate on those goals. If we needed money to get something for Kathleen's diabetic care, I'd make sure we'd have it. And we still intended to live a full and joyful life with our family and not to lose sight of our other dreams. Nevertheless, Jeanne and I needed to discuss how we were going to "jump" the latest "hurdle" in our lives while keeping our attention focused on the finish line.

Think Long-Term Gain, Not Short-Term Pain

Some IBOs may be tempted to rationalize that it's okay to quit running after their dreams and drop out of the hurdle race... that it's okay to take a "wrongful life settlement" because there are a lot of people worse off than they are.

Hey, they're probably right. Things could be a lot worse, I suppose. But it's been my experience that people who give up on their dreams end up regretting it. Interviews with residents in nursing homes indicate that most people don't regret what they DID in their lives. They regret what they DID NOT DO!

Don't make the mistake of missing out on living your dreams because you made a wrongful life settlement in the short term. All too often the short-term pleasure leads to long-term disaster.

Being contented with the short-term results reminds me of the comment made by pitcher Warren Spahn of the Milwaukee Braves after he served up a pitch that Willie Mays smashed for a 400-foot home run. When a reporter asked Spahn what he thought of his pitch, Spahn remarked, "For the first 60 feet, it was a beautiful pitch."

Same thing happens in our lives when we think short term instead of long term. For the first few years, things may be beautiful, indeed. But then reality steps up to the plate in the form of layoffs... or illness... or injury... and smacks our smugness right out of the ballpark!

Oh, by the way. Warren Spahn went on to pitch another day. He didn't quit baseball because of one setback. In fact, Spahn went on to win a total of 363 games and was voted into the National Baseball Hall of Fame in 1973.

Just goes to show you that whether you're playing baseball or building The Business, you're going to have some home runs hit against you, even when you make the perfect pitch. But always remember, in the end, the winner is the one who stays in the game and *does whatever it takes to realize his dreams!*

Fill in the Gaps

Formal education will earn you a living. Self-education will earn you a fortune. You will determine how much of a fortune you will earn by how much self-education you decide to get.

–Jim Rohn
professional speaker

Some friends of mine own a consulting/training firm. They meet with company managers to find out what their employees need to know, then my friends test the employees to discover where the gaps are in their skills and knowledge. Once my friends understand what the employees need to learn, they design training systems to "fill in the gaps."

Filling in the gaps is what personal growth is all about. You may have gaps in your education. Or gaps in your communication skills. Or gaps in your leadership ability. But no matter what gaps you have in your personal and professional life, it's up to YOU to fill in the gaps, not someone else.

It's like the story of the father who sat down with his son to have a heart-to-heart talk about the boy's poor grades.

"Son," said the father soberly. "I'm worried about your being at the bottom of the class."

"Don't worry, Dad," replied the boy nonchalantly. *"They teach the same stuff at both ends."*

The boy is right—the students at both ends of the grading scale have access to the same information. The "A" students and the "F" students hear the same lectures and are issued the same textbooks. When all is said and done, it's the student's responsibility to fill in the gaps by learning the material.

Same goes for The Business—it's up to you to identify the gaps and fill them in.

Why Invest in Yourself and Your Business?

Everybody in The Business wants to get something out of it. That's obvious. But all too many IBOs want to get something *out* of the business without putting something *into* the business.

Sorry, life doesn't work that way. Before you can *take out,* you have to *put in.* Before you can drink from the glass, you have to fill it up. Before you can take withdrawals OUT of your checking account, you have to put deposits IN. It doesn't get any more basic than that!

Successful companies go out of their way to help employees fill in the gaps by offering comprehensive employee training programs. Smart companies understand that employees are their most valuable assets. Upper managers know from experience that the companies with the most knowledgeable, best-trained employees are the ones who will prevail in the marketplace. End of story.

Daniel Burres, a highly respected futurist, tells a great story about a CEO he met who didn't want to spend money on training.

"What happens if I spend a lot of money training my employees and then they leave me?" asked the CEO.

"What happens if you don't spend the money and they STAY?" replied Burres!

The same is true for YOU and your business. What happens if you try to "save" money and time by choosing NOT to invest in your business? I'll tell you what will happen—either you'll fail and DROP OUT of The Business. Or, worse yet, you'll STAY in The Business and make everyone else on your team miserable—*including yourself!*

The Size of Your Gap = The Size of Your Dream

How much time and money do you need to invest in your business? The short answer is that it depends on what you want out of The Business (remember, you can't take *out* more than you put *in*).

If all you want out of The Business is a few hundred dollars per year, then you'll need to make a smaller investment than if your goal is to grow your business into a full-time career. It stands to reason that if you have a

HUGE dream—and I hope you do—then you probably have a HUGE gap to fill. So, plan on making a commitment to invest whatever it takes in time, money, and effort to make your dream come true!

Look at the diagram below. It shows the gap that exists between what you WANT in life... and what you HAVE right now.

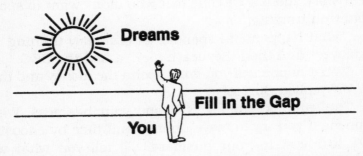

The more you invest in your business, the smaller the gap becomes. It's that simple. If you want to become a high-priced attorney, for example, you have to fill in the gap by investing your money and time going to college for four years... then law school for three years... and then you *still* have to work long hours as a low-paid associate for three to five years to prove you're worthy of becoming a partner in the firm. (If that's not enough, once the firm accepts you as a partner, you have to invest as much as $100,000 or more to become an equity partner.)

Whew! It takes a lot of money, a lot of time, and a lot of effort to fill in the gap enough to become a successful lawyer. With that kind of investment, it makes you wonder why there are so many lawyers....

Granted, doctors and lawyers have to make huge investments of time and money before their gaps are filled in, but the truth is, every profession or business requires *some* investment of time, money and effort, including The Business. There's no such thing as a free lunch. If you want to become free, you must fill in the gaps by investing your time and money learning The Business while you build your organization from the ground up.

Three Types of Gaps

Okay, we've established that if you want to be successful in The Business, you've got to fill in some gaps. As I see it, there are three major types of gaps separating your HAVES from your WANTS. The three major gaps are Knowledge Gaps, Belief Gaps, and Action Gaps. Let's take a closer look at each one.

1. **Knowledge Gaps:** When you first start out in The Business, you don't know much about the product line... or how to do The Business... or how to build business builders. This shouldn't be surprising. NO ONE is really prepared to become successful in The Business until they are actually in The Business. All your life, you've been trained to work in a job and trade your time for money. You didn't go to trade school or college to learn how to build The Business, so you need to invest some time and money acquiring the basic KNOWLEDGE and KNOW-HOW.

2. **Belief Gaps:** Most new people are convinced The Business works, but very few new people are convinced THEY can work The Business. Little wonder. Most people associate with average Joes who aren't particularly successful and don't have a true understanding of what it takes to BECOME successful. Most people don't have a needle on

their internal compass that always points north to success. Before you can become successful, you need to BELIEVE in The Business and in yourself... and then you need to help your teammates fill in their belief gaps—NOW!

3. **Action Gaps:** You can have all of the knowledge in the world... and you can have the STRONGEST belief in The Business and its ability to set you free... but if you don't take ACTION, nothing will happen. How many talented, inspiring, and just plain LIKEABLE people do you know who just won't get started? What're they waiting for? Are you one of those people who say, "I'll get started just as soon as I learn a little more"? But, all too often, people NEVER get what they want because they simply won't take action. You need to invest in ACTIONS, or you'll never get results.

Great Business Builders are BUILT, Not Born

It's difficult to look at hugely successful IBOs and imagine that they, too, had gaps that needed filling before they could enjoy the fruits of The Business. Today, they're polished, professional, and, well, wealthy. But, when they first started in The Business, many of them had HUGE gaps that needed filling in. When you hear their stories, it's hard to believe they knew so little. How could they have built such fantastic businesses—and built such fantastic business builders—if they were so inexperienced and ill prepared? The answer is, they paid the price and made the investments necessary to fill in the gaps.

The simple truth is that successful people do what unsuccessful people refuse to do. When successful people need more knowledge, they make sure they get it! They read the books and listen to the tapes that fill in their knowledge gaps. If they need more belief, they surround themselves with positive, successful people so that it becomes IMPOSSIBLE not to believe. And, if the LACK OF ACTION is what separates their haves from their wants, big business builders simply step up and take action— again and again—as often and as much as it takes! They don't wait around until they have perfect information or perfect belief. They simply DO IT! Instead of "ready, aim FIRE," the slogan of successful business builders is "FIRE, ready, aim!"

Can't Count on College to Fill in the Gaps

Do you remember what business you're *really* in? You're in the business of building business builders, isn't that correct? But when you joined The Business, did you know how to build business builders? Has anything in your past trained you to do that? Did you ever take a course in school that taught you the Art and Science of Stimulating the Human Spirit?

I can testify from personal experience that no such course exists! I've been teaching for 20-plus years, and I've yet to see a college course dedicated to personal growth. Nowhere in the educational system is there ANYTHING about building business builders to achieve financial freedom.

How about on your job—do they bring in consultants to train you how to build business builders? Is there a program at your company that leads to financial freedom? Is your boss constantly saying, "Please tell me your wildest, most motivating dreams so that we can show you how to reach them"? No way!

So, if nothing in life has prepared you to succeed in The Business, you'll need to learn some things about building business builders. Before you can grow your business, you'll need to GROW as a person and as a leader.

Enrolling in the College of The Business

As I pointed out, you can't count on college to fill in the gaps. So, how do you get the information and training that you need to become successful in The Business? Well, instead of enrolling in a business college, I suggest you enroll in the College of The Business, better known as The System.

The System is designed to give you the information, knowledge, know-how, and tools to help you succeed. Just as a college education imparts knowledge and know-how to its students through teachers, classes, and textbooks, the College of The Business imparts knowledge and know-how to the IBOs through live functions, tapes, books, and tools.

Now, let me ask you a question. When someone goes to college, does the college pay them? Or do they pay the college? They pay the college, of course! The students willingly INVEST in their college education and, in return, they get knowledge and know-how. No one is forced to go to college. Students pay of their own free will. Does that mean every person who pays for a college education becomes a success? No. College degrees don't come with guarantees, do they?

Same goes for the College of The Business. Think of plugging into The System as an INVESTMENT in acquiring the knowledge and know-how that will help you succeed in The Business. Does anyone force you to pay for the information? Absolutely not! Does every IBO who invests in The System become a success? No. Just as college degrees don't come with guarantees, neither does The System guarantee that you'll build a profitable business. But I can guarantee you this. Not every IBO who plugs into The System will build a profitable business... but *every IBO who is running a profitable business is plugged into The System!*

The Low Cost of Learning

Look, the point I'm making is that everything comes with a price. As I tell my marketing students, price is what you have to give up to get what you want. If you want to grow in The Business, you have to give up some money, time, and effort. End of subject.

Compared to the start-up costs in a traditional business, investing in The Business is ridiculously inexpensive. *But the failure to invest in The Business could cost you a fortune!* If you don't take the time to invest in knowledge, belief, and actions, your business will not grow. Which means you'll always be separated from your dreams—and the cost of that is HUGE. It means you had the opportunity of a lifetime, but because you didn't make the investments to fill in the gaps, your opportunity will never be realized. That's what Ben Franklin would call being "penny wise and pound foolish." Without investing in personal growth, your future will be the same as your past—that is, you'll keep on getting what you've always gotten until the day you stop working! Then, your future will be WORSE than your past, as your income dwindles while your expenses remain the same.

How Much Are You Investing in YOU?

As a teacher and consultant, I meet and talk with hundreds of new people every year. One thing I hear over and over again is that most people are frustrated. They feel like underachievers. They know they're settling for less, and they don't like it! They want to HAVE more and BE more, but they just don't know where to begin.

I tell them to begin by investing in themselves because that's the best investment they'll ever make. I tell them to fill in the gaps by reading books. Listening to tapes. Attending live seminars and events. Talking with mentors. Fill in the gaps FIRST, I tell my students and clients, and everything else will fall into place.

I'll close with a quote from one of the giants in the personal growth movement. I'm hopeful that the quote will challenge you to re-evaluate your commitment to filling in the gaps in your personal and professional life:

> *"General Motors invests over a billion dollars annually on research and development. May I respectfully inquire how much time and money you, as a person, are investing in your own research and development this year?"*
>
> —Earl Nightingale

Believe You Can Achieve!

People will sit up and take notice of you if you will sit up and take notice of what makes them sit up and take notice.

–Frank Romer

Like most families, we occasionally get behind schedule and are forced to run out and grab some fast food for dinner. One evening, Jeanne came home with our bags of burgers and told me about a sign she'd seen posted on the door of the employees' entrance. The sign was placed there to motivate the employees. It read:

T.E.A.M.

Together, Everyone *Accomplishes* More

Ironically, we had just seen a similar sign from a group in The Business that read:

T.E.A.M.

Together, Everyone *Achieves* More

Now, at first glance, there doesn't seem to be much difference between the two signs. The verb in the first sentence says "accomplish." The verb in the second sign says "achieve."

But on closer inspection, you'll see that this subtle difference in the wording of a motivational sign explains the monumental difference between people who work for others in a job... and people who are working for themselves in The Business.

Take a moment to read the signs again! Now ponder the difference between the two words, "accomplish" and "achieve." Put the book down and take a few minutes to see if you can list any differences between the two words. List them in the columns below:

Achieve	vs.	Accomplish
Def: *To attain by exertion*		Def. *To complete a task*
1.		
2.		
3.		
4.		
5.		

To help you make a distinction between the two words, I've listed some differences that occurred to me. Before you read my list, however, I want to remind you that I've been a college professor for 20-plus years. I've taught literally thousands of students during that time. At the end of each semester, my job is to assign each student a grade from "F" to "A."

Now, after they receive their grades, a student or two will invariably challenge the grade I gave them. Almost without exception the challenge will come from "C" students who want to know why they got a "C" instead of an "A" or "B."

"I did all of the assignments," they'll say with exasperation. "I attended all of the lectures. I took all the tests. Why did I get a 'C'? I deserved a better grade!"

It's been my experience that the BIG difference between the "C" students and the "A" students in college—and in life—is the "LITTLE" difference between the meaning of the words *accomplish* and *achieve.* In a nutshell, the difference is that accomplishers get it done. *Achievers get it done RIGHT!*

With that in mind, let's take a look at my list comparing achievers to accomplishers:

Achievers	vs.	Accomplishers
Def: *To attain by exertion*		Def. *To complete a task*
1. Gives maximum effort		Gives required effort
2. Passionate about their work		Goes through the motions
3. Committed to excellence		Committed to getting it done
4. Always self-motivated		Sometimes motivated by others
5. Paid what they're worth		Paid what the job is worth
6. Reach for the stars		Settle for what they can get
7. Do more than the job requires		Do the minimum
8. Dream oriented		Task oriented
9. Whatever-it-takes attitude		Do-just-my-job attitude
10. Get what they want		Get what the boss gives them

Accomplishers Take What the Job Gives Them

We hear the expression, "over-achiever" a lot these days. Ever hear the expression "over-accomplisher?" No, and you won't, because it would be a contradiction in terms. Accomplishers don't over-anything. They just do enough to get the job done.

The sad thing about accomplishers is that they'll never get more out of life than what someone else will give them. It reminds me of a joke a friend of mine who used to work for the government likes to tell.

"Do you know the most dangerous place in the world?" he asks.

"The parking lot of a state office building at 4:30 in the afternoon!"

If you've ever lived in a state capital or worked for the state, the joke really hits home. "Quittin' time" is 4:30 PM sharp, and when the clock strikes 4:30, it's like the running of the bulls in Pamplona. Stampede to the parking lot!

That's because the vast majority of government employees are accomplishers, not achievers. All too many of them have an employee mentality: "I'll trade the minimum amount of hours and effort for the maximum pay and benefits."

Now, don't get me wrong. I'm not saying every government employee is a slacker. Not true. There are some real go-getters in every profession. But compared to the private sector, government jobs generally offer low pay but LOTS of security. So, naturally, the kind of people who seek government jobs are more concerned about security, benefits, and a pension than anything else. That's why there are no shortages for applications for government jobs. Accomplishers line up to apply for government jobs like the Green Bay Packers fans line up for season tickets. Sad, but true.

Achievers Get What They Want

Okay, we've established that accomplishers get what the job gives them. What about achievers? ACHIEVERS are different. Achievers get what they WANT!

You see, *achieving something means you decided what you wanted first, then found a way to go and get it.* The way to achieve time and money freedom is to be an Independent Business Owner. Because IBOs are BUILT, not hired and trained, die-in-the-wool accomplishers need not apply! You need to be an achiever to do The Business because there's no one standing over your shoulder telling you exactly what to do. BUT the rewards you reap for achieving in The Business are so much greater than the rewards you'd receive for accomplishing as an employee.

Ask yourself, "What do I really WANT? Do I want to be an employee? Or do I want to be FREE? Do I want to work my way up to a manager of employees who will help me 'make my numbers' for the year? Or do I want to build business builders who will help me reach my dreams for a lifetime?"

If you're in The Business, I know how you answered those questions—you want to be free! You want to reach your dreams. Now, let's turn to Business Basic #6 and learn how to make it happen!

Find Out What Your Partners Want... Then Help Them Get It!

The most important single ingredient in the formula for success is knowing how to get along with people.

**–Theodore Roosevelt
26th U.S. President**

What makes a great manager of people? Fats Waller, the legendary blues singer and songwriter, said it best:

"Find out what they want, and then give it to 'em jus' that way!"

Waller's advice may sound simplistic, but it's the single biggest motivator of people. Some people want more money. Some people want more freedom. Some people want more recognition. Some people want to be on the stage. Some people want to be behind the scenes. The list goes on and on. The key to building a successful business is to find out what everyone on your teams wants, and then show them how The Business can satisfy those wants.

You see, unlike traditional businesses, The Business isn't about YOU. The Business is about YOUR PARTNERS! People who think The Business is about them reminds me of the joke about the college professor who was returning from a trip with several graduate students. The professor was one of those self-centered know-it-alls. For the first two hours of the trip, he did all the talking—and all he did was talk about himself! Finally, he got tired of talking and announced, "Okay, I've talked about me long enough. Now it's your turn to talk about me." No one likes people like the college professor because they only care about themselves. There's a saying in The Business. "No one cares how much you know until they know how much you care." So true!

That's why it's so important to discover people's wants. It shows you care. Research proves that people will work harder for something if it gives them exactly what they want. If you bought a new car, for example, would you be satisfied if the salesperson said, "You'll get the next car off the assembly line. I don't know what color it'll be or what options it'll have, but it'll be yours because you're caller number 332." You'd feel offended, wouldn't you? Disrespected. Why? Because that's not the car you want! When you buy a new car, you shop around, looking for the one with all the goodies that make you beam like a kid at Christmas. If the dealer doesn't have the car on the lot, you order the one you WANT!

Remember the gifts you got on your last birthday? Which shirt is your favorite? Is it the polyester Hawaiian shirt you got from Aunt Sarah who was shopping for Uncle Eddie and just happened to find a two-for-one sale? Or is it the one you really wanted—the 100% Egyptian cotton with monogrammed cuffs in just the right color that you ordered for yourself online from your OWN store? We both know the answer to that question...

Do you know what everyone likes more than getting something at a cheap price? *Getting exactly what they want!* If you're serious about building business builders, you have to learn to *customize* so that your teammates and clients get *exactly* what they want.

What Do Business Builders Want?

There's only one way to find out what other people want. Ready? You have to ASK them! This, unfortunately, involves a skill that most of us have never really learned. It's called LISTENING!

Most people's wants can be broken down into seven categories. I call them the "Seven Rs." They are Rewards, Recognition, Relief, Rejuvenation, Respect, Relationships, and Reduced Risk.

How many and how much of the "Seven Rs" someone wants and when they want them is a matter of individual preference. If you want to become a master business builder, you need to understand each of the Seven Rs and learn how to find out which ones your people want most.

Let's take a brief look at each of the Seven Rs:

1. Rewards: This is the category that most people respond to initially. Many Independent Business Owners build their businesses for the rewards they receive. It could be money... or the things money can buy. It might be a new home, a boat, college tuition for their children, etc. Or, the rewards could be less tangible, such as a feeling of accomplishment. In any case, rewards are the easiest category to work with because you can get the other person talking about what they want.

Clue words: "Someday, I'd like to have...."

2. Recognition: I loved being a Boy Scout because of the merit badges. Every time I would complete the requirements for a badge, there was a little ceremony at the Scout meeting, and I'd receive my badge in front of the whole troop. When I completed a major milestone, there was a BIG ceremony. I was recognized along with other scouts who had also "made the grade." I dreamed of the day my uniform would be covered with badges! Those were the days.

So, now that you're a grownup, do you ever get special recognition at work? If you are recognized, it's probably for making the company more money. When was the last time you got rewarded at work for achieving a personal dream? Probably never. Likely, your boss's unwritten rule is keep your work life and your personal life separate. Sure, you may be recognized for being a better customer server. Or for having perfect attendance. Or for selling the most cars for the month. But no one at work recognizes you for achieving a dream, do they!

Are you beginning to appreciate the power of The System? When someone walks across the stage, they're being applauded by people in The Business for what they've ACHIEVED in The Business. They get to brag to the audience about how The Business has enabled them to realize their personal dreams! Not work-related goals. But PERSONAL DREAMS! That's a powerful motivator.

In The Business, your work and your personal life are one and the same. The Business isn't just a way of making money—it's a way of living!

Clue words: "I like what I do, but I wish someone would NOTICE it and say 'thank you.'" Or, "Sure I want more money, but what I REALLY want is for my family to be proud of me."

3. Relief: Sometimes, you just want the struggle to be over. Wouldn't it be a relief NOT to worry about finances? Who wouldn't want that kind of relief? Let's face it, almost everyone works hard for a living, but for most people, there's just no relief in sight. Most people earn just enough money to pay the bills, which means they'll be working hard for the rest of their lives! What if you could show them how they could work a little harder for a few years, but then STOP working, or STOP worrying, for the rest of their lives? If that doesn't get them excited, check their pulse. They may be dead! Work with your people to bring them relief and show them how to help others.

Clue words: "I just can't seem to get ahead."

4. Rejuvenation: Why do people take vacations? The answer is supposed to be something like, "to recharge their batteries and get a fresh outlook." But for most people, a vacation is an escape from the day-to-day struggle they go through at work. Instead of taking a break to become refreshed, most people look at vacations as "the only time when they can't reach me at work." Well, that's a terrible way to live. And it's DEFINITELY a reason to build a big business.

Use the rejuvenation "Hot Button" to get your people FIRED UP about The Business. Business builders stay motivated because they're constantly finding new and interesting things to do. Working with people who are discovering their dreams, possibly for the first time, is very exciting.

Clue words: "I just can't seem to get excited about things at my job." Or, "I love the weekends because that's MY TIME!"

5. Respect: It's impossible for me to hear the word "respect" without thinking of two things – Aretha Franklin and her song, "R-E-S-P-E-C-T" and Rodney Dangerfield with his classic line, "I don't get no respect." Both refrains conjure up the same image. We're all looking for a little respect!

Well, new people in The Business are no different—they want respect, too. That's great! But in The Business, respect isn't just a birthright—it's earned! Help your partners learn how respect is earned in The Business so that they, too, can enjoy the positive feelings that go along with being respected. Show them that in The Business, they have to match their actions with their words if they want respect. They have to respect the leaders and their accomplishments before THEY can become leaders themselves. And most of all, they have to respect The Business in order for The Business to respect them!

Clue words: "Most people don't listen to my ideas. I'm trying to do my best."

6. Relationships: I'm a man, so relationships are a difficult subject for me to talk about. When it comes to sharing my feelings, I'm definitely Old School. I avoid it at all costs. I'm a man, so I'm from Mars. However, I live in a house full of females from Venus—my wife, two daughters and even a female dog named Koko. I'm learning to speak Venusian—fast!

Actually, I do know something about building relationships. Jeanne and I have been married for 17 years, and we're happier now than ever before. I'm proud of our relationship, and both of us work hard to keep it strong and vibrant.

It's no coincidence that so many of the leaders work The Business as a couple. Why? Because building a better relationship with your spouse goes hand in hand with building The Business. As I said earlier, working The Business isn't just a job. It's a lifestyle! And building relationships is a biggest part of building a successful life.

Not long ago, a young couple asked Jeanne and me, "What makes your relationship so strong?" My answer was immediate.

"I'm physically afraid of Jeanne," I said straight-faced. "And that keeps me from doing stupid things." Well, the young man and I had a good laugh, and then we both ran to do the dishes while Jeanne and the young man's wife sat around and had coffee.

Just kidding! Here's the real answer: The key to our great relationship is trust. I can trust Jeanne to do what she says she'll do. I can trust her to be a great mom to our two daughters. I can trust her to provide wise counsel. And most of all, I can trust her to be my best friend. Likewise, Jeanne can trust me to pull my weight. She doesn't have to second-guess me because I don't give her a reason to.

I trust Jeanne because she's consistent. Consistency is a rare commodity these days. You can depend on a consistent person. You aren't worried about them not doing what they say they're going to do or flying into wild moods. It makes everything easier, and then—and this is the part that men have a problem with—then you can open up to each other and SHARE stuff.

So, consistency leads to sharing and sharing leads to a deeper trust and dependence. It works in a marriage, and it works in business. Stephen Covey, author of *Seven Habits of Highly Effective People*, calls this "interdependence." Look around at the most successful business builders, and you'll observe that the bigger the pin, the better they are at building lifelong interdependent relationships.

Clue words: "It would be great to find some other people who have goals like me," or "Where can I meet some positive people who KNOW where they are going?"

7. Reduce Risk: Risk is something that most people really don't understand. They want to avoid risk as much as possible. Yet risk is necessary for success. Where there is risk, there are rewards.

However, in working with business builders, you can give them what they really want—reduced risk—by helping them build their businesses fast. You need to be a good example of risk management, not risk avoidance.

Interestingly, some of the other Seven Rs will reduce risk. Great REWARDS certainly make up for any risk a business builder undertakes. And RECOGNITION and RELATIONSHIPS are two fundamental risk reducers. Your consistency and friendship may be the only commodities needed to bring peace of mind.

Clue words: "I don't like taking chances." Or, "What will people think of me?"

Okay, So What DON'T People Want?

If the Seven Rs are all things that your business builders want, what *don't* they want? Well, the people who you're looking for—the big builders—don't want what they already have. They want change, and they want it now.

They're "sick and tired" of being sick and tired. They know that the job or profession they're working in now isn't going to help them reach their dreams. So, they want to move forward, not stay in the same place.

More than anything else, here's what they don't want: *They don't want to be treated like employees!* They've already been there, done that. And got the tee-shirt to prove it. Now, here comes the hard part. New IBOs don't want to be treated like employees, but they don't know how to be their own bosses! So you have a balancing act. You have to transition them from the employee mindset... to the entrepreneur mindset. From the *dependent* business worker, to the *Independent* Business Owner.

So take Fats Waller's advice and "find out what your IBOs want, and then give it to 'em jus' that way" (that is, give them the gift of independence). I assure you, they'll be singin', all right. *But they'll be singin' your praises instead of the blues!*

Look for Big Problems (That's Where the Big Profits Are!)

The basic problem most people have is that they're doing nothing to solve their basic problem.

—Rev. Bob Richardson

Here's a story that illustrates why it's better to look for problems and confront them head on rather than trying to avoid them. The story goes like this:

An old farmer owned a large field. It was the most fertile field in the county except for one problem—*right in the middle of his field was a huge rock!* Over the years, the rock had been an endless source of aggravation to the farmer. Seemed that every spring the farmer would break a plow on the rock. All told, that big rock had cost him dozens of plows and thousands of dollars in lost labor.

One day, after breaking another plow, the farmer decided he'd had enough. He marched to the barn and grabbed a big crowbar. He placed the crowbar under one side of the rock and pulled back with all his weight. He was astonished to feel the big rock move!

The farmer worked his way around the edge of the rock with his crowbar. What the farmer thought was an immovable boulder turned out to be a slab of rock less than a foot thick! By the end of the day, the farmer had broken the rock up and hauled it away in his wagon. Not only did he remove the rock, he used it to build a wall to keep the neighbor's pigs out of his wife's vegetable garden!

Moral of the Story

When we avoid problems, they sit in the middle of our lives like a big rock in the middle of the farmer's field. The only way to make our problems go away is to attack them head on. (And more times than not, the problems that seem so big turn out to be much smaller than we thought.)

Problems! Problems! Problems! We've all got our share of problems. And, yes, it's a lot easier to avoid our problems than it is to attack them head on. But the truth is, big problems offer big opportunities. That's why I tell my students and clients to *look for big problems because that's where the profits are hidden!*

Think about it. In the 1950s and '60s, the pace of American life increased dramatically. Suddenly, millions of people had a big problem—there wasn't enough time to get things done! But this big problem created even bigger opportunities. McDonald's offered "fast food" for time-starved workers. Pizza Hut responded to hungry, harried households by delivering dinner right to the door! Microwaves and automatic dishwashers became standard household appliances. Thousands of time-saving devices flooded into the marketplace (remember "stay-pressed pants" that didn't require ironing?), and lots of companies made lots and LOTS of money solving the big problem of people having too much to do and too little time to do it.

Look for Problems—Then Offer a Solution

Problems—who needs 'em? YOU NEED THEM! Why? Because problems are where the profits are! You have to understand this concept in order to operate a successful business. You see, in business you either solve people's problems or you don't stay in business. It's that simple.

My dad is old enough to remember the days when the iceman would stop at his parent's home every day and drop a big block of ice in the icebox. This solved the refrigeration problem in everybody's home. Ice companies made a lot of money back in those days, and being an iceman was a steady, dependable job.

Then everybody got electricity and iceboxes were replaced by electric refrigerators. No more iceman stomping around the kitchen every day. No more melting ice all over the floor. Electric refrigerators solved the refrigeration problem more efficiently and more economically than iceboxes. The ice makers went out of business, and George Westinghouse and dozens of other electric refrigerator manufacturers got rich.

This pattern of one solution being replaced by a better solution has been repeated millions of times since the Industrial Revolution. Mousetraps were invented to solve the problem of mice scurrying around the house. Solve people's problems by building a better mousetrap, and they'll beat a path to your door.

High Pay Can Lead to Huge Problems

Did you ever ask yourself why people even bother to work? So they can make money, correct? Why is money so important? Because people need money to buy products and services to solve their problems. After people solve their basic problem of food, shelter, and safety, they start looking around for other problems to spend their money on. They pay people to mow their yards. They pay people to groom their pets. They pay people to clean their houses. They pay people to wash their cars. They pay people to cook their meals. The list goes on and on. When you think about it, that's all the economy is—people paying for products and services that solve their problems.

It stands to reason that the bigger the problem, the bigger the opportunity. So the question becomes, what are the biggest problems people face today? The answer is obvious: Lack of time and lack of money.

Truth is, almost everybody faces the twin problems of too little time and too little money. Even most high-income people aren't immune to these problems. As an example, let's look at an attorney who makes $100,000 per year.

Now, a hundred grand is a lot of money. Most people would LOVE to make that kind of money. "All my problems would be over if I made that kind of money," most people would tell you.

But the attorney knows otherwise. Here's why. In order to earn his $100,000, the attorney has to work AT LEAST 50 hours per week—and 70-hour weeks are the norm when one of his cases moves to trial.

What are some of the problems our high-paid attorney has, and what CAUSES those problems? Well, this man has two primary "problem causers" in his life. First, he has a lack of time. He's in the office for about 10 hours a day. He also has to commute to and from work, and he takes work home on occasion. So, he has little time to do all the things that he needs to do to keep his life in balance. He seldom sees his kids' baseball games. His wife is angry most of the time because he's seldom home. By the time he gets home, he's so tired and stressed out that all he wants to do is park in front of the TV and vegetate. Which leaves the kids and the wife feeling even more neglected.

His second big problem is money. *He doesn't have enough of it!* He earns $100,000 a year, but after taxes, his TAKE HOME PAY is $5,800 a month. Which means after paying the mortgage on a $250,000 home... car payments on two late-model imported cars... and tuition for three kids in private school, well, there's nothing left at the end of the month. He badgers his kids to make good grades so they'll get college scholarships because there's no money set aside for college. To complicate matters, he's TERRIFIED that the money will stop coming in if he got sick or lost his job.

The System Solves the Problem

Can you help the attorney solve his problem of too little time and too little money? Absolutely! You simply show him how residual income generated by The Business can give him more money and more time to enjoy it! Problem's solved!

You see, folks, you're perfectly positioned to solve all kinds of problems by simply applying the basics of your business. The Business is designed SPECIFICALLY to solve these problems. You don't have to create new solutions or do anything fancy. Just apply the proven, basic principles to solve people's little problems ("I don't have time to run to the store for toothpaste and toilet paper all the time"), as well as their big problems ("I'm tired of living paycheck to paycheck").

One of the basics to building The Business is to help people solve their problems... and then do it again and again. The beauty of The Business is that if your partners learn how to solve enough little problems for other people—such as saving them time by having soap and toothpaste delivered to their door—then their big problem of not having enough time or money will take care of itself!

The Power of PROVEN Problem Solving

The best thing about The Business is that the products and services, as well as the business model itself, have been proven. The products work. The System works. The Business works. There's a 50-year track record of proven problem solving. And I can testify from personal experience that a PROVEN product and business model count for a lot!

In 1984, my wife and I started a computer software company. We created a computer game that trained people how to respond to emergency situations. One version was *Hotel Fire!* The simulation exercise ran on a personal computer, and the participants were put into fire-related situations and asked to choose courses of action to help save lives and property. It was a great program that certainly would help solve a serious problem—how to train hotel personnel to react properly if there were a fire.

We invested all of our extra money into the project. We borrowed more money and invested that. We sold stock in the company. We were passionate about our product. We worked hard to make the business succeed. However, after a couple of years, our business went belly up! Why? Because in 1984, very few employees had access to personal computers! We discovered the hard way that we were WAY AHEAD OF THE CURVE! We were so cutting edge that we cut ourselves right out of the market!

It took us five years, but Jeanne and I paid back all the investors—every dime! We learned a valuable lesson from that whole experience. The lesson was about as basic as it gets. *Before you start trying to solve people's problems, make sure your product or service does just that.*

Our product didn't solve people's problems because the rank-and-file employee couldn't access our information. You see, our product and business model was unproven. We walked out on the tightrope without a net. We tried to INVENT a product and a business. That can be done—just ask Bill Gates. But it's awfully tough! Gates has admitted that luck has played as big a role as hard work and skill in his climb to the top.

The beauty of The Business is that the pioneers have already blazed the trail and settled the land. All you have to do is follow their map. The difference between starting up a new business with new products and starting The Business is the difference between walking alongside Lewis and Clark during their exploration of the Louisiana Territory and traveling to the west coast in an air-conditioned Mercedes via the Interstate. *No comparison!*

Paradigms vs. "Para-dollars"

No doubt you've heard the word "paradigm" before. It's a big buzzword in all the business books. A paradigm is a way of thinking or acting. Essentially, a paradigm is a set of beliefs.

The paradigm for The Business has been around for years, but it's still viewed with suspicion. The prevailing business paradigm in most people's minds is "go to school, get a good job, retire with a pension when you're 65." Only one problem. That paradigm hasn't worked since the Eisenhower years—and that was over 40 years ago!

All you have to do is pick up a newspaper to see that the old business paradigm isn't working. The old get-a-job paradigm was supposed to offer job security for the workers. But that paradigm doesn't favor the workers anymore. That paradigm favors the owners and shareholders! That's why companies lay off thousands of workers at the first hint of a downturn—the CEO wants to protect the value of the stock. (He also wants to protect the value of his stock options, but that's another story.)

I have a saying: "Why settle for a paradigm when you can have a para-dollar?" In other words, why settle for the insecure paradigm of earning a fixed monthly salary in a job... when you could be enjoying a proven "para-dollar" of earning unlimited residual income in The Business?

As I said earlier, the reason people take jobs is to help them solve their problems. If you don't have any money, you can't buy groceries or pay rent, can you? So people grab onto the conventional paradigm—they jump on the job bandwagon. And for a while, the job paradigm works pretty well. That is, until the kids come along. Or the company you work for hires a tyrant of a boss.

Truth is, the job paradigm works pretty well for people with dime-sized dreams. But what about people who have dollar-sized dreams? Or million-dollar-sized dreams? Does the old job paradigm work for them? Does it solve their biggest problems of lack of time and lack of money? No. There are lots of talented, ambitious people looking for an opportunity that will solve their BIG problems of not enough time and not enough money. The old get-a-job paradigm won't solve their problems. And they know it. They need a new residual income para-dollar solution.

That's where you come in. Do your friends and acquaintances a favor and show them how you can help them solve their biggest problems. Show them they don't have to settle for an old paradigm... when they could have a new para-dollar.

Duplicate, Don't Negotiate!

You don't get the breaks unless you play with the team instead of against it.

–Lou Gehrig
legendary baseball player

I recently read an article in the "My Turn" section of *Newsweek* magazine that made my blood boil. The "My Turn" essay features a different essay each week from ordinary people with, presumably, something of value to say.

This particular article was written by a high school teacher who was commenting on the $100 million long-term contract signed by Derek Jeter, the All-Star shortstop of the New York Yankees. The teacher claimed he didn't begrudge Jeter the money but suggested that Jeter should donate a huge portion of it to build a public school so that teachers could do a better job. The next week, many readers wrote letters to the editor saying what a great human being this teacher was and how we needed more people like him in the world.

What are these people thinking? Who are they to tell an *achiever* like Jeter what he should do with his money? The teacher and his admirers sum up the philosophy of the Entitlement Age: "Taking is more noble than making."

Nonsense! The day every American agrees that siphoning off wealth is more noble than creating wealth is the day that former Soviet leader Nikita Khrushchev's prophecy, "We will bury you," will be fulfilled. If the Age of Entitlement grows unabated, the Russians won't have to bury us. We'll bury ourselves!

Duplicate, Don't Negotiate!

Here's why the *Newsweek* essay made me so furious:

Let's start our discussion with the subject of the article, Derek Jeter. Here's a person with enormous talent. But, having talent isn't all that's needed to play in the major leagues. Derek Jeter has dedicated his life to the pursuit of his baseball career. Sure, he's talented. But he's also DRIVEN! And DISCIPLINED!

Truth is, there are THOUSANDS of people with talent, but most don't WORK to hone their skills to the point where they can succeed at the professional level. Jeter is so good that he makes the game look easy. But he got that good by practicing the basics of his craft over and over again. Jeter just happens to ply his trade in a marketplace that pays top performers millions of dollars a year. Good for him.

Now let's look at the high school teacher who thought Jeter should donate his money to helping the less fortunate. The teacher spent time in the column talking about how little money he made. Yet, he felt good about himself because he was helping others. The teacher said he didn't make enough money to build a school, so he wanted Jeter to subsidize it. (Ever notice how much easier it is for people to spend other people's money on "good causes" rather than their own?) It was bad enough that the teacher was so misguided. What really sent me over the top was that so many readers thought the teacher was so noble.

Give me a break! Since when is mooching noble? What kind of lesson is this high school teacher actually TEACHING our children? In effect, he's delivering this message to our children: "Be poor, because poor is more noble than rich. Then, look for people with money and try to get them to feel guilty enough to give you some of it."

I tell you, folks, this is just the opposite of the lesson I want my children to learn. I don't want my kids to copy what poor people do so that they'll have to beg rich people for handouts. I want my kids to copy what rich people do so that they'll be financially independent. In a word, I don't want my kids to *negotiate* with successful people for contributions, I want them to duplicate successful people! I say, *Duplicate, don't negotiate!*

If this high school teacher wants to have money AND be noble, there are plenty of examples for him to follow. Why can't he do like YOU are doing? Why not learn to work as a teacher AND own a low-risk, high-ethics, wealth-producing business that grows and helps people achieve their dreams? If building a school is **his dream**, why not find a way to make that dream come true through free enterprise, rather than begging? Aren't there plenty of people in The Business who have achieved their dreams through hard work? You bet!

The Difference Between Do-ers... and Do-Gooders

Look, I don't mean to imply that I'm against teachers or non-profit organizations. I'm a teacher, too, you know. Been teaching college for 20-plus years. But I'm also a speaker, trainer, consultant, author, investor, and business owner. I don't think of myself as a do-gooder. I think of myself as a do-er who happens to teach.

Teaching is something I enjoy. And, yes, I suppose I "do good," at least according to some of my former students who tell me I did a good job preparing them for their business careers. But you'll never hear me berating Bill Gates for not donating money to my university. Gates earned his billions, and he's earned the right to spend his billions as he sees fit. As for "giving back to the community," well, Gates is "giving back" billions every year in the form of taxes while employing THOUSANDS of workers all over the globe. That's the kind of giving back I'd love to see more of! I tell my students that if they really want to make a contribution to humankind, then duplicate the success of Bill Gates. If they do one tenth of one percent as well as "Dollar Bill," then they'll enrich the lives of hundreds, if not thousands, of people.

I'd be the first person to tell you that we need ALL kinds of people in this world. We need teachers and social workers and volunteers for the American Cancer Society and staff workers for the United Way. I give my share of money to non-profits every year, and I'm delighted to have the financial wherewithal to help out those less fortunate than I.

But the way I see it, the "do-gooders" in the public sector, such as teachers, have no business telling the "do-ers" in the private sector, such as professional athletes and Independent Business Owners, what they should do with their money. Get real!

Let's face it—the do-gooders owe their existence to the do-ers, not vice versa. The real heroes in this world are the people CREATING WEALTH, not the people CONSUMING WEALTH. The do-ers, such as yourself, are the ones creating wealth. Without you do-ers, there wouldn't BE any do-gooders. Why? *Because there wouldn't be any money to pay them!*

The Power of Duplication

When I say, "Duplicate, don't negotiate," I mean that people should *duplicate* what wealth creators DO so that even more wealth will be created, instead of *negotiating* with the wealth creators for "donations" and "gifts."

If more people duplicated what the do-ers DO, then more people would have what the do-ers HAVE. This isn't rocket science here. This is just good old common sense. The power of duplication can be summed up by the billionaire oil man J. Paul Getty, who said, "If you want to get rich, find someone who is rich and do what he's doing."

Great advice. So the question becomes, "What is it exactly that do-ers do that makes them so successful?"

Now, it's pretty obvious that there's a zillion things a person can do to create wealth in this world. Derek Jeter is creating wealth by playing baseball. I have good friends in dozens of different businesses who are creating LOTS of wealth for themselves and their families: They're restaurant owners... publishers... real estate owners... software developers... business consultants. The list goes on and on.

But have you ever noticed that do-ers may have vastly different God-given talents, and be working in vastly different fields, but without fail, do-ers share certain "success traits" in common? Do-ers will tell you that their "success traits" are the real secrets to their success, because they empower the do-ers to create wealth when many of their cohorts are struggling to make ends meet.

If people could be taught these "success traits," they'd stand a much better chance of becoming successful themselves, wouldn't you agree? Years ago, the leaders in The Business recognized the same thing, namely, that the best business builders shared certain "success traits" and that teaching these traits to others increased an IBO's chances for success. Recognizing the power of duplication, the leaders put together a system to teach others the traits for success. Today, this success system is known simply as The System.

So, What Is The System?

The System is a duplicatable method for business builders to show other business builders how to succeed. That's the sole purpose of The System—to help people build up themselves so that they can become better business builders.

The System is composed of a growing inventory of knowledge, wisdom, beliefs, attitudes, and know-how designed to help people succeed in The Business and in life. The wealth of information in The System comes in many forms—audio and video tapes, books, literature, CD ROMs, and live events, to name a few. When you plug an

IBO into The System, it's like plugging a light into an electric socket—*the juice flows and the light goes on!*

There's a saying in The Business. "Not everyone who plugs into The System is a success. But everyone who is a success plugs into The System." That's so true. Look at any successful enterprise. Their success comes from developing a duplicatable system and then working that system over and over again. Businesses with lousy systems don't stay around very long, do they?

Remember when I said, "Duplicate, don't negotiate"? Well, this advice applies to The System as much as it does to wealth creation. Some people try to negotiate with The System:

"I'll listen to the tapes, but I don't need to go to meetings anymore," they may say. Or, "Instead of doing The Business like my mentor tells me, I'll try a new angle he hasn't thought of." That's negotiating with The System. And it's courting disaster! Don't negotiate—DUPLICATE! Like the TV commercial for AT&T used to say, "The system is the answer." The System is made up of methods that work. If something doesn't work, it doesn't get into The System. Period! The leaders selecting the material for The System have been in The Business for years... decades, even! They've seen it all. If it works, they've done it. Your job isn't to invent a better system. Your job is to COPY a proven system!

McDonald's: Where Would They Be Without The System?

Look at any successful chain store or franchise, and you'll see that the "secret" to their success is a tried and proven system. Wal-Mart and The Home Depot don't have a thousand different accounting systems in a thousand different stores. They have one that works! And that's all they need! The system is the answer.

For example, McDonald's gives franchisees a cookie-cutter system. All new franchisees need to do is follow the proven system that has made thousands of other franchisees successful. Nothing is left to chance at McDonald's. They may have the worst hamburger in the fast food industry, but they have the best system—BY FAR! As a result, McDonald's is far and away the most successful franchise in history. That's the power of putting a duplicatable system in place.

What do you think McDonald's headquarters does with franchisees who "negotiate" with the system by, say, using their own recipe for the french fries or substituting soy burgers for the hamburgers shipped to their store? McDonald's Corporate would boot 'em out of the business quicker than you could say Ronald McDonald, that's what they'd do!

Well, mavericks aren't necessarily booted out of The Business—they end up booting themselves out of The Business. People who refuse to plug into The System don't get results, so they quit! IBOs pay a high price for choosing to "go it alone" in The Business. It's called failure!

It Depends on What You Want

There are certain things you have to do to become successful in any business. That's just the facts. The Business is no different. If you do what The System tells you to do and keep repeating it over and over, you'll become a do-er. End of story.

The next time you're thinking about negotiating with The System, think of this story: Two men are watching the Tour de France bicycle race on the television.

"I don't understand why they would do that," said the first man.

"Do what?" asked the second man.

"Put themselves through three weeks of torture," replied the first man. "The contestants pedal more than 2,000 miles, suffering through grueling mountain climbs, slogging their way through rain and sleet one day, only to encounter blistering sun and heat the next. Why would anyone put themselves through that?"

"Well, the winner gets millions of dollars in endorsements and prize money," said the second man.

"Oh, I understand why the WINNER would do that," said the first man. "But why would those OTHER GUYS go to all that trouble?"

Ladies and gentlemen, life is like the Tour de France. We all have mountains to climb and valleys to navigate. But for the winners, it's worth it! The beauty of The Business is that there's more than one winner! Don't think of The Business as the Tour de France where ONE WINNER gets all the spoils. Think of The Business as the Tour de Globe, where THOUSANDS of people will EARN MILLIONS OF DOLLARS while the race is still going on!

When you're tired and your spirit is down, you'll be tempted to negotiate with The System by taking a shortcut: "I'll just go to bed early instead of going to the meeting tonight. I've worked hard and I deserve a break," you may negotiate.

But remember, *winners don't negotiate.* Winners DUPLICATE what every winner before them has done.

Winners stay the course.

Winners trust The System.

And winners keep on pedaling!

If you do that, you'll be a winner. And once you cross the finish line, you, too, will be able to say, "Oh, NOW I understand why I did that. *That's what winners do, and I'm one of them!"*

Plan Your Work... and Work Your Plan

I am a friend of the workingman.
And I would rather be his friend than be one.

–Clarence Darrow
American lawyer

Julio Melara, one of the top-paid keynote speakers in the world, never fails to tell his audiences about the present he received from his mother for his 10th birthday.

Julio had opened all of his other presents when his mother presented him with "the best present of all." Julio smiled and tore off the wrapping paper to discover a wood box with these hand-painted letters on the top:

"THE SECRET OF SUCCESS"

Julio stared at the lettering. Just what he wanted—*the secret of success!* Julio dreamed of the day he could drive a new car and move into a big home. This box held the key to all of his dreams!

Julio lifted the lid and peered inside to see a piece of paper with a one-word message:

"WORK!"

No Shortcuts to Success

The message to 10-year-old Julio must have stuck. Julio went on to become a successful business owner and a world-renowned speaker and trainer. He credits his success to his mother's guidance and solid values. Work wasn't a four-letter word in the Melara household. Work was a virtue to be honored and respected.

Julio understood at a very early age that there are no shortcuts to success. Oh, sure, as he got older he worked smarter. Instead of delivering newspapers as he did as a child, Julio OWNED a newspaper as an adult. But he got to the top by WORKING SMART AND HARD.

In my opinion, we need more people like Mrs. Melara in the world—people who understand the correlation between work and getting ahead in the world. Used to be that people just ASSUMED they'd have to work hard to make something of themselves. But in the Age of Entitlements, more and more people are taking the attitude that LIFE OWES THEM A COMFORTABLE LIVING.

Today, all too many parents would put a different message in the box labeled, "The Secret of Success." Instead of WORK, the message would read, "SUE SOMEBODY!"

Where did we go wrong?

Not All Plans Are Created Equal

Like Julio, I'm a big believer in work. Work is where the rubber meets the road. But hard work by itself isn't enough to guarantee success. I know lots of people who are hard workers. But the sad truth is, no matter how hard most of these folks work, they'll never achieve the Ultimate Goal of time and money freedom. Why? Because *they're working the wrong plan!* If you work the wrong plan, then no matter how hard you work, you'll never achieve the results you're after.

Here's an example of what I mean:

Several years ago, I had a new swimming pool put in. It was the middle of summer in Florida—92 degrees with 80% humidity. The sun was relentless. A crew labored from six in the morning until six in the evening. I tell you, the guys who did the job WORKED for their money! It took these guys a month to put in the pool. When they got done, they went to their next job. I went for a dip in my new pool.

It occurred to me that while these guys were grunting and sweating in the hot Florida sun, I was sitting in my air-conditioned home office typing on my laptop. Cold glass of lemonade next to the computer mouse. Leaning back in my ergonomic chair while I worked.

The pool builders and I were working for the same basic reason—we wanted to earn money for ourselves and our families. But we were working very different plans! Their plan was to *trade their time for money* by installing swimming pools in people's backyards. And they worked HARD at their plan. My plan was to *create residual income* by writing a book that, hopefully, thousands of people would buy. And I worked HARD at my plan.

Now, I ask you, whose plan for earning money do you think is working better? Their time-for-dollars plan? Or my residual income plan? Better question: *Whose plan would YOU like to work?*

Here's my point: **Not all plans are created equal!** Even though time-for-money plans and residual income plans both require hard work, only the residual income plan can lead to the Ultimate Goal of time and money freedom. Yes, hard work is indispensable for success. But working hard at the wrong plan will just leave you frustrated. And bitter. *And broke!*

10-Step Plan for Success

I tell my students and clients that there's a time-tested, fool-proof, 10-step plan for success. The 10-step plan goes like this:

Step 1:   Make your plan.

Step 2:   Make sure your plan works.

Step 3:   Work your plan.

Step 4:   Work your plan.

Step 5:   Work your plan.

Step 6:   Work your plan.

Step 7:   Work your plan.

Step 8:   Work your plan.

Step 9:   Work your plan.

Step 10:   Work your plan.

So What Is This Thing Called "a Plan"?

Here's my simple definition of a plan:

A plan is a series of actions you take to achieve your dreams.

That's ALL a plan is. A plan is simply a means for organizing your activities. A well-written plan is a blueprint for achieving your dreams. Nothing more. Nothing less.

Making a plan that works and then WORKING that plan is a basic of business. In fact, at first glance, it seems SO BASIC that even a child would understand it. Yet most people fail either to plan their work *effectively...* or to work their plan *effectively.* Studies show that people spend more time planning their vacation than they do planning their retirement. Now, how smart is that? A vacation lasts two weeks. A retirement lasts 20 years. Yet most people spend more time planning their vacation? Scary, isn't it?

Two Pitfalls to Planning Your Work and Working Your Plan

What's so hard about developing a plan that works and then working that plan? Well, as a consultant, I've pondered this question for years. I've seen hundreds of business plans over the years. More often than not, they fail. What goes wrong? It seems so simple—draw up a plan, stick to it, and get the results you want. What could be easier?

If it were only that simple.

I read recently that on any given day, one-third of American adults are on a diet. That's about 50 million people who plan to lose weight. *Yet only 2% of dieters lose their target weight and keep it off for more than a year.* Which means there are LOTS of people making plans, but very few people getting results.

As I see it, there are two major reasons plans fail:

One, the plan has a fatal flaw.

Two, the person executing the plan has a fatal flaw.

Let's take a moment to discuss each of these pitfalls so that YOU know how to avoid them as you're drawing up and working your plan for success.

Flawed Plans Get Flawed Results

I'm amazed at the flawed business plans that get "green-lighted." The recent fallout on the Internet is a perfect example of what I'm talking about. The dot.com bomb was ignited by dozens of seriously flawed plans. Ever hear of Value.com? Talk about a flawed plan that did NOT work and will not work—ever! The business plan for Value.com was to attract millions of customers by selling products BELOW COST and then to make money by selling advertising to companies that wanted to reach those millions of customers. In other words, Value.com set out to *intentionally* LOSE MONEY ON SALES on the hopes they would MAKE MONEY ON BANNER ADS. Is that dumb, or what?

Now, lots of stores will occasionally sell a popular product at a loss in order to sell other products at a profit. It's called a "loss leader." A drugstore, for example, might advertise quarts of Coke for 50 cents, even though it costs them 60 cents to buy it. They'll lose 10 cents a quart. But the store will make their 10 cents back AND THEN SOME when they sell the Coke shoppers dozens of other products at full retail.

Offering occasional loss leaders is a good business plan. Basing your entire business model on a plan to sell products for less than you paid for them isn't a good business plan—IT'S SUICIDE! Talk about a flawed plan. This one ranks up with the plan to put screen doors in submarines as the business plan most destined to fail!

Value.com ignored Step 2 in the 10-Step Plan for Success: *Make sure your plan works.* Value.com's plan didn't work. Will not work. Cannot work. In fact, the Value.com business plan was SO FLAWED that the better the company got at making the plan work, the deeper in debt they got! Value.com was working a built-in plan to self-destruct. Dumb. Dumb. Dumb.

Planning to Spend Themselves into the Poor House

I'm appalled at the number of business plans that don't have a chance of working. But for every business that is working a flawed plan, there are *thousands of citizens working hopelessly flawed business plans!* The business plan that most Americans are working goes like this: Get a job. Get two to four paychecks totaling X amount of dollars each month. And then spend X+Y supporting your lifestyle.

This business plan is as flawed as Value.com's—there's more money going out than coming in. So, what do

Americans do? Rather than throwing out their flawed business plan, they try to tweak it. They start buying more and more stuff AT DISCOUNT, justifying their spending by telling themselves they're "SAVING" money every time they buy a product at, say, a 20% discount. It's insane! When people buy a $100 product at a 20% discount and pay "only" $80 for it, they didn't "SAVE" $20. They just SPENT $80!

Simple truth is, people who buy at deep discount aren't saving money—what they're really doing is spending themselves into the poor house! Case in point: According to *Newsweek* magazine, the average American family carries $8,000 in credit card debt. *But spending is still on the rise!* Talk about a prescription for disaster!

The American Bankruptcy Institute recently reported *that bankruptcy filings shot up 25% in one quarter alone,* the highest quarterly total ever! "The figures are alarming," said Samuel Gerdano, the institute's executive director. *Newsweek's* cover story "Maxed Out" sums up our out-of-control credit card culture with this headline: "Freud could have a field day analyzing the denial and the rationalization that underlie our *relationships with credit cards.*"

The Business Plan of The Business

Remember my definition of a plan: *A plan is a series of actions you take to achieve your dreams.* Well, the actions most Americans are taking—get a paycheck and then spend all of it PLUS SOME MORE— can't help them achieve their dreams. I understand that different people have different dreams, but I assure you, suffocating under a mountain of debt is NOT the American Dream!

Folks, the spend-more-than-you-make-by-buying-at-discount-and-charging-it plan isn't working. Can't work! It's seriously flawed. Wake up, America! Instead of a "relationship with credit cards," what people really need is a relationship with EACH OTHER!

Now, compare the flawed business plan that millions of Americans are working... to the business plan of The Business. Day and night difference. You see, the business plan of The Business creates wealth by rewarding people for buying smarter, not cheaper, and then teaching others to do the same. It's what I call "pro-suming."

Pro-suming is a combination of producing and consuming. It's the best of both worlds. Producers make money. Consumers spend money. Pro-sumers make money while they spend! Pro-sumers create wealth by buying smarter, not cheaper, and teaching others to do the same.

The pro-sumer-based business plan of The Business works... but only if you work the plan! Remember the *10-Step plan for success:*

Step 1: Make your plan.

Step 2: Make sure your plan works.

Steps 3-10: Work your plan... work your plan... work your plan....

Let me repeat—*the business plan of The Business works!* The proof is evident in the tens of thousands of Independent Business Owners who are creating wealth and living debt free by buying from themselves at "My-Mart.com" instead of Wal-Mart or Kmart... and teaching others to do the same.

On the other hand, the conventional business plan of buying at discount with a credit card that millions of Americans are following is seriously flawed. American consumers are drowning in debt by trying to "save" money by buying at deep discount. They need rescued! They need a lifeline! They need someone to show them a different business plan... a proven plan that will give them a series of actions so that they can achieve their dreams... a business plan that works so that they can work the plan and get the results they want—time and money freedom!

Working Your Plan

Okay, so we agree that not all plans are created equal, isn't that correct? And we agree that the first pitfall to Basic #9: *Plan your work and work your plan* is that the plan may have a fatal flaw. In the case of most Americans, the business plan they're working is so flawed that it's not only NOT helping them achieve their dreams—*it's taking them in the opposite direction. It's burying them deeper in debt!*

The second pitfall to planning your work and working your plan is that the person working the plan may have a fatal flaw. Now, at first glance, it would appear that most people who work good plans and get bad results have BIG FLAWS. But that's not the case. Most people getting bad results are no different from you and me. They aren't necessarily less intelligent. Or incompetent. More often than not, their failure to get the results they want comes from their *lack of productivity,* not their lack of ability.

You see, there's a BIG DIFFERENCE between *activity and productivity.* Successful people recognize this and spend *80% of their time being PRODUCTIVE* and only 20% being active. Unsuccessful people working the same plan spend *80% of their time being ACTIVE* but only 20% being productive.

The best way to explain the difference between activity and productivity is to tell you about a Realtor friend of mine. My friend is a top-producing Realtor. He's made well over 100 grand a year for 20-plus years selling homes. My friend classifies his work time into one of two categories: It's either "A" time or "F" time. "A" time is the time he spends face to face with a client, either getting a new listing for a home or selling a home. Everything else is "F" time.

In other words, "A" time is the time spent being PRODUCTIVE. "F" time, on the other hand, is the time spent being ACTIVE. Are you beginning to see the difference? Being productive in the real estate business means SELLING HOMES! Realtors are independent contractors. In effect, they're Independent Business Owners, correct? So if they don't sell homes, they don't pay the bills. No sales, no income. No income, no food on the table. End of subject.

So, in order to be a successful Realtor, you HAVE to be productive. So, my friend avoids "F" time like the plague! If he has paperwork to fill out, he delegates it to his secretary. Yes, paperwork has to be completed. But paperwork doesn't PAY. Therefore, paperwork is "F" time to him. He understands that only "A" time pays. So my friend delegates EVERYTHING he can every time he can. He's a delegating machine! As a result, he's been a top producer year after year, in good markets and bad. My friend is successful and he's achieving his dreams because he practices the basics: He plans his work... he has a plan that works... and he works his plan!

Working the Plan vs. Working AT the Plan

Working The Business is like working as a Realtor in that you're on your own in both industries. No boss to tell you what to do. No way to "fake your way through the day" and still get a full paycheck at the end of the week (as so many employees are accustomed to doing). In both real estate and The Business, only the producers make money. So it's imperative that you understand the difference between *productivity*... and *activity.*

Productive IBOs work their plan. Over and over again. Because they work their plan, they get results. They grow their business. And they make money.

Active IBOS, on the other hand, work AT their plan. They tell others (and themselves) they're working their plan. But they're not. They're working AT their plan by spending time tinkering with the "F"-time tasks of The Business.

For example, IBOs who work AT the plan will spend their weekends building shelves in their garages to store their products. IBOs who work AT the plan will spend hours in front of their computers customizing spread sheets to keep track of their home-based businesses. IBOs who work AT the plan will spend their evenings organizing their business files and sorting their product literature into neat stacks. Are they active? You bet. Are they busy? Sure are. Are they organized? Yep. *Are they productive?* **NO!**

My editor faxed me a syndicated cartoon from the funny pages of the local newspaper that points out the difference between activity and productivity. The cartoon is called "Pickles" by Brian Crane. In this particular series,

Mrs. Pickles, an older lady who is a bit eccentric, is standing next to a plant in her living room. She's holding a watering can and looks to be watering the plant.

"What are you doing, Mrs. Pickles?" says a little neighbor girl.

"Watering my plants, Gina," replies Mrs. Pickles.

"But they're artificial plants," says the little girl with a confused look on her face.

"I know, dear," replies Mrs. Pickles. "But it doesn't matter. There's no water in the watering can anyway."

You see, Mrs. Pickles is being active. She's doing something. She's working AT watering her plants. But she's *not being productive* because no plant is actually benefiting from her actions.

What about you—is your business benefiting from your actions on a daily basis? Are you being productive? Or just active? Are you working The Business? Or working AT the business? Are you planning your work and working your plan? Or are you just planning your work... and planning your work... and planning your work... and never really getting around to WORKING YOUR PLAN?

As I said earlier, not all plans are created equal. The business plan of The Business, for example, is certainly UNEQUAL! Why do I say that? Because the business plan of The Business is designed to create unlimited residual income. Do the work once and get paid over and over again.

Now, I ask you, is that a great plan? YES!

Does the business plan of The Business work? YES!

Are tens of thousands of people all over the world achieving their dreams by working the business plan of The Business? YES!

One final question: Is the business plan of The Business working for you?

I'd love to answer this question with a resounding YES, also. But the truth is, I can't answer the question for you. The only person who can answer the question, "Is the business plan of The Business working for you?" is... you.

If the answer is "no," then I urge you to get back to Basic #9: *Plan your work and work your plan.* If you do that, I guarantee you that a year from now your answer will switch from a timid "no"... to a resounding **"YES!!!!"**

Add Value to Everything You Do!

*In the end, all business operations
can be reduced to three words:
People, products, profits. People come first.*

–Lee Iacocca

Let me tell you another story—this one true. Not long ago, while on vacation, I was playing golf. There was no breeze, and the sun was beating down from a cloudless sky. It was hot, really hot. It was going to be a long day on the links.

We had just reached the fifth tee, which was at one end of the course. Across the street was a small development of houses. It looked like some kids had set up a table with coolers nearby.

"Want some ice-cold lemonade, mister?" The question came from a skinny boy about 12 years old.

"Wow, that sounds really great," I said. Before I had even finished the sentence, he handed me a small glass of pink lemonade. It looked cold and refreshing.

"How much?" I asked.

"One dollar," he replied.

"A dollar for a glass of lemonade?!! That's *really* EXPENSIVE," I protested.

"Well, this is made fresh with real lemons," he said. "I mix it up by the glass. You'll really enjoy it. And there's nothing better than fresh ice-cold lemonade on a hot day like this."

I wasn't convinced. Then he delivered his closing line.

"If you a buy a glass here, I'll come find you on the 12th green and bring you another glass way over there. Anyone who buys a glass from me is a regular customer."

"How much will the second glass cost me?" I asked, enjoying his spirit of free enterprise.

"Another dollar, but I'll run it over to you so it'll be really fresh and really cold!" he offered.

I bought the lemonade—both glasses. The lemonade didn't help improve my golf game, but it sure improved my mood! How much was that lemonade worth to me— especially that second glass? It was worth a lot more than a dollar!

That kid taught me a valuable lesson. He wasn't afraid to ask for a good price. He didn't flinch when I questioned him. And instead of lowering his price, he found ways *to increase the value of his product.*

You see, folks, he didn't want to sell lemonade at 50 cents a glass. He wanted to get a full dollar for it. So, he had to find some way to increase the price while still making his customers happy. How did he do it? He added value.

He could have reduced his costs by using a lemonade mix instead of real lemons, but his profit margins wouldn't have been as high. So, he decided to make it fresh—AND CHARGE MORE. He could have just sat behind his table and let the customers walk over to him. But, that wouldn't bring a premium price. So, he DELIVERED it—and he ran instead of walked.

This young man *added value,* and that value represented benefits to me. He kept on adding value until the benefits were greater than the money I was paying for them. He got his price, and I got a lot of refreshment and a good story. We were both happy with the transaction.

Business Is a Food Chain

No doubt you've heard of the food chain. Little stuff is on the bottom of the food chain and big stuff is on top. Well, the product cycle is just like the food chain. Every product starts with raw materials (the little stuff), and then, as the product moves up the chain, the price keeps getting bigger and bigger until the consumer eventually buys the finished product (the big stuff).

People can make money ANYWHERE along the product chain by simply adding value and then passing it on at a higher price. Take a car, for example. The bodies are made out of steel. A mining company removes the iron ore from the ground and delivers it to the steel maker for, say, 10 cents a pound. The steel maker melts it down and presses it into sheets which it sells to a car manufacturer for $1 per pound. The car manufacturer molds the steel into a car body, and then sells the steel in the new car body to consumers for the equivalent of $10 per pound.

There might be 20 links along the chain where a vendor or broker or manufacturer or distributor will add some value and make some profits. That's the way the value-added business chain works.

Do most people like paying $20,000 for a brand new car? No. Do most people think that cars are overpriced? Yes. But let me ask you a question: Which would you prefer driving around town?—an unpainted hunk of iron with folding chairs instead of cushioned seats for $10,000? Or a shiny, new Toyota Camry with leather seats for $20,000?

Considering the Toyota Camry is the best-selling car in the world right now, I think it's safe to assume that consumers may grumble about the sticker price for a new Camry, but in the end, they're willing to pay the price because they think it's a great value!

In the business chain, you pay a little more for a product or service each time someone adds value, but it's worth it. You're not just buying the product—you're also buying distribution, information, convenience, service, and guarantees. All of these things cost money, but in the long run, the extra money you pay equals the value you get.

And, that's the whole secret to the business chain. You can put yourself ANYWHERE in the chain and make a profit, as long as three things happen:

1. You add value.
2. You sell the stuff for MORE THAN YOUR COSTS.
3. The next person in the line KNOWS and APPRECIATES the value you added.

That's it. That's business in a nutshell—add value and then sell it for a fair and reasonable profit to someone who recognizes and appreciates the full value of the product. And, in that regard, The Business is no different than any other business.

Handling Two Common Objections

I'm often asked to give speeches on my book, *Pro-sumer Power.* Without fail, someone looking at The Business will approach me after a speech and make one of two comments:

"I don't like the idea of making money from my friends."

or

"The products are too expensive. Why don't they reduce the prices and make The Business a big discount buying club?"

Most likely you've heard these objections, as well. Comments like this come from people who don't understand two basics of business: One, the predominate purpose of business is to make a profit; and two, *it's smarter and more profitable to increase value rather than lower prices.* The best way to overcome the objections that "the products are too expensive" is to add so much value that people don't even question The Business model or the price of the products (we'll discuss the kinds of value you add in a moment).

As for the objection that IBOs are making money on their friends, I say to people, "I'd rather my friends made money on me than someone else. I have friends who sell insurance and real estate, and guess who I call FIRST when I need insurance or want to sell my home? MY FRIENDS! There's absolutely NOTHING WRONG with making money from your friends if you solve their problems and add value!"

In Order to Have Profit-Sharing, You Have to Have Profits!

The Business works on a system of profit-sharing. That's why profits are so important. Without profits, there's nothing to share and no reason to stay in business.

There are two things that affect the size of the profits: costs and price. Take a manufacturer that makes shirts, for example. The owners are in the shirt-making business for one primary reason—they want to make money. In their case, they make money by making shirts for X (the costs) and then selling them for X + Y (profits).

Consumers can get those shirts through retail stores. Or they can get them through The Business. The shirt company doesn't care how the shirts are distributed. Are there differences in distribution costs between a retailer and The Business? Sure there are! The retailer has tons of expenses you don't have, such as buildings, employees, advertising, etc. But the retailer has two big advantages you don't have. One, big retailers buy in BIG volume, which means they can buy and sell products cheaper than you can. And two, consumers are conditioned to buy from stores, so when they need a shirt, the first thing that pops into their mind is, "I need to drive to the store and buy a shirt."

A big part of your job is to educate people about the advantages of shopping from home. Once they understand the benefits of online shopping, they won't automatically jump in the car and head to the store. Instead, they'll boot up their computer and order the products. You see, you can get the money the retailer would have gotten if they had made the sale. *But you only get the money if you add value.*

Opportunity: The Ultimate Added Value!

Let's continue this discussion of how you can add value by first looking at how the world's biggest retailer, Wal-Mart, adds value. Why is Wal-Mart so successful? It's certainly not because of their great service, that's for sure! The key values Wal-Mart adds are lots of locations and the lowest prices in town. And how do they keep those prices so low? Three ways: One, they buy in huge volume. Two, they keep their overhead down—Wal-Mart has very plain stores with little decoration. And three, they staff their stores with a skeleton crew of minimum-wage clerks. When you shop at Wal-Mart, you're pretty much on your own. Big volume, low overhead, and minimum service—that's how Wal-Mart keeps their prices so low.

But, as I said earlier, you don't want to compete with Wal-Mart. They're in the DEEP DISCOUNT retail business, and they're so good at what they do that they're pushing other retailers right off the map. Montgomery Ward, a century-old company with hundreds of stores across North America, was the latest casualty of the retailing wars. While Montgomery Ward is shuttering their stores and filing for bankruptcy, Wal-Mart continues to open hundreds of new stores every year around the world.

So, if you can't compete with the Wal-Marts of the world on price, what do you do? What value do you add that Wal-Mart can NEVER add? Well, for starters, you can add great service in the form of convenience and product knowledge. Anyone who has ever shopped at Wal-Mart knows that service is w-a-a-a-a-y down on their list of priorities. I don't know what's worse when I shop at a Kmart or Wal-Mart—not being able to find a clerk. Or finding one! I cringe every time I track down a clerk because I end up helping them more than they help me!

So, convenience and product knowledge are definitely two ways you add value to the price of your products. But there's one more thing of value you add that all of the Kmarts and Wal-Marts can NEVER add. What's that? Opportunity!

Opportunity—there's that word again. But what a powerful word it is. And it's the single reason the prices of the products and services in The Business are fair and reasonable, *even if that very same product is available somewhere else for 20% lower—or even 50% lower, for that matter!* Let me explain:

American Dream Based on Opportunity, Not Lowest Prices

To fully understand the awesome value of opportunity, let's go back in history to the colonization of North America. The vast majority of North Americans descend from immigrants, correct? According to the bestselling book, *The Millionaire Next Door*, the largest ancestry group in North America come from German immigrants, followed by English, Irish, French, Italian, and Dutch. Now, why did people from all over the world scrimp and save their pennies (or worse, indenture themselves as servants working for free for up to seven years) so that they could spend four months herded like cattle in the steerage of a leaking ship in order to settle in a land they'd never seen?

One reason and one reason only—*opportunity!*

Millions of people didn't emigrate to America because the prices of groceries and housing were lower in New York than in, say, Sicily or a small Irish village. No way! In fact, the first thing an immigrant would notice was the high prices in America—OF EVERYTHING! Whether it was food, clothing, housing... *everything cost 10... 20... 100 times what it would have cost in their homelands.* Talk about sticker shock! That's why at the turn of the 20th century, two, three, four families were packed into one-room apartments throughout Manhattan, Brooklyn, and the Bronx.

So, once the immigrants discovered the high cost of living in North America, did they complain to their friends, "America needs to lower their prices or I'm going back home"? Did they return to their homelands in droves because the cost of living was cheaper where they came from? Not in a million years!!! You see, even the illiterate, unsophisticated immigrants understood the added value of living in North America. *They eagerly adjusted to the high prices of everything because opportunity was added into the prices!*

My ancestry on both sides is from Ireland. My dad remembers his father telling him about signs posted outside stores and taverns saying, "No Dogs, No Irish." In

New Orleans just prior to the Civil War, 20,000 Irish camped on the banks of the Mississippi in living conditions worse than livestock. Most of the Irish immigrants were unemployed. Those who got work were paid 50 CENTS A WEEK as maids and stable hands. Did the Irish immigrants seek to return to Ireland, where the standard of living was a fraction of what it was in the States? Not on your life. The Irish and every other immigrant group stayed in a hostile land where everything was ridiculously expensive because *they understood that the ultimate value—opportunity—was added into the price of every product and service.*

But most of all, the immigrants in North America remembered that in their former homelands, where EVERYTHING WAS CHEAPER, there was no opportunity to create wealth for themselves and their family. No opportunity to advance out of their social class. No opportunity to grow as a person. No opportunity to become free. And most of all, *no opportunity for them or their children to own their own lives and create their own destiny!* In short, every immigrant understood that the cost of staying in their homeland was FAR HIGHER than the cost of emigrating to America. Because America offered *opportunity, they came here by the millions!*

You're an Opportunity Store

Do you remember Business Basic #3: "Know Your Competition"? You're not in competition with Wal-Mart's low prices—*you're in competition with people's low expectations!*

Think of The Business as America and your prospects as immigrants. You've got what they need—opportunity!

Your prices may be higher than the prices they pay in their "homeland" (Kmart's slogan is, "Where America shops"). But so what?!!! In 1900, bread was 10 times cheaper in Europe's Italy than it was in New York's Little Italy. Yet Italians and millions of other immigrants kept coming to these shores in waves! Ellis Island processed 22 million European immigrants between 1892 and 1924. Why? Because America was known all over the world as the *Land of Opportunity, not the Land of Deep Discounts!*

"If you want to have more, then think like a store," I said in *Pro-sumer Power!* Well, you need to think like an OPPORTUNITY store, not a discount store! Your products and services cost what they do because you're adding the greatest value of all—opportunity!

Think about it! Your opportunity can change people's lives. Wal-Mart can't do that. Your opportunity can help people get out of debt. Wal-Mart can only help people STAY IN DEBT. Your opportunity can help people get what they want most in life—more time and more money. Wal-Mart takes people's time and money!

So, don't THINK like a discount store. Think like an OPPORTUNITY STORE that's going to add value and charge a fair and reasonable price for your products and services. Because you have no physical store, big inventory, or other major distribution costs, the discount store's EXPENSES become YOUR PROFITS! The manufacturer still makes their profit. You make your profit. And your client gets more value. You're simply "in the product development chain," adding value and creating profits. But never, ever lose sight of the fact that priced into your products is the ULTIMATE VALUE— OPPORTUNITY.

Why Do You Think It's Called "The Business"?

I shouldn't have to say this because it's so obvious. But for some reason, the obvious just flies right over some people's heads. Here's the obvious point that so many people miss: *Don't be ashamed or afraid of making profits. Be PROUD of it!*

It's called The Business for a reason, folks.

It's not called The Government Handout.

And it's not called The Non-Profit Group.

It's called THE BUSINESS.

As President Calvin Coolidge observed, "The business of America is business." If you don't believe Coolidge, just look at what happens to countries (and people) who don't believe in for-profit business. They end up like the old Soviet Union—broke and miserable and hopeless!

The problem with Russia today is that the business of Russia is bureaucracy, not business. The business of Cuba is oppression, not freedom. Thank God the business of America and dozens of other freedom-loving countries is business.

Freedom and free enterprise go hand in hand, folks.

I wouldn't want it any other way, would you?